Marcellina Oseghale Akpojotor

Marcellina Oseghale Akpojotor

ΓΕΛΕ

SKIRA

Summary

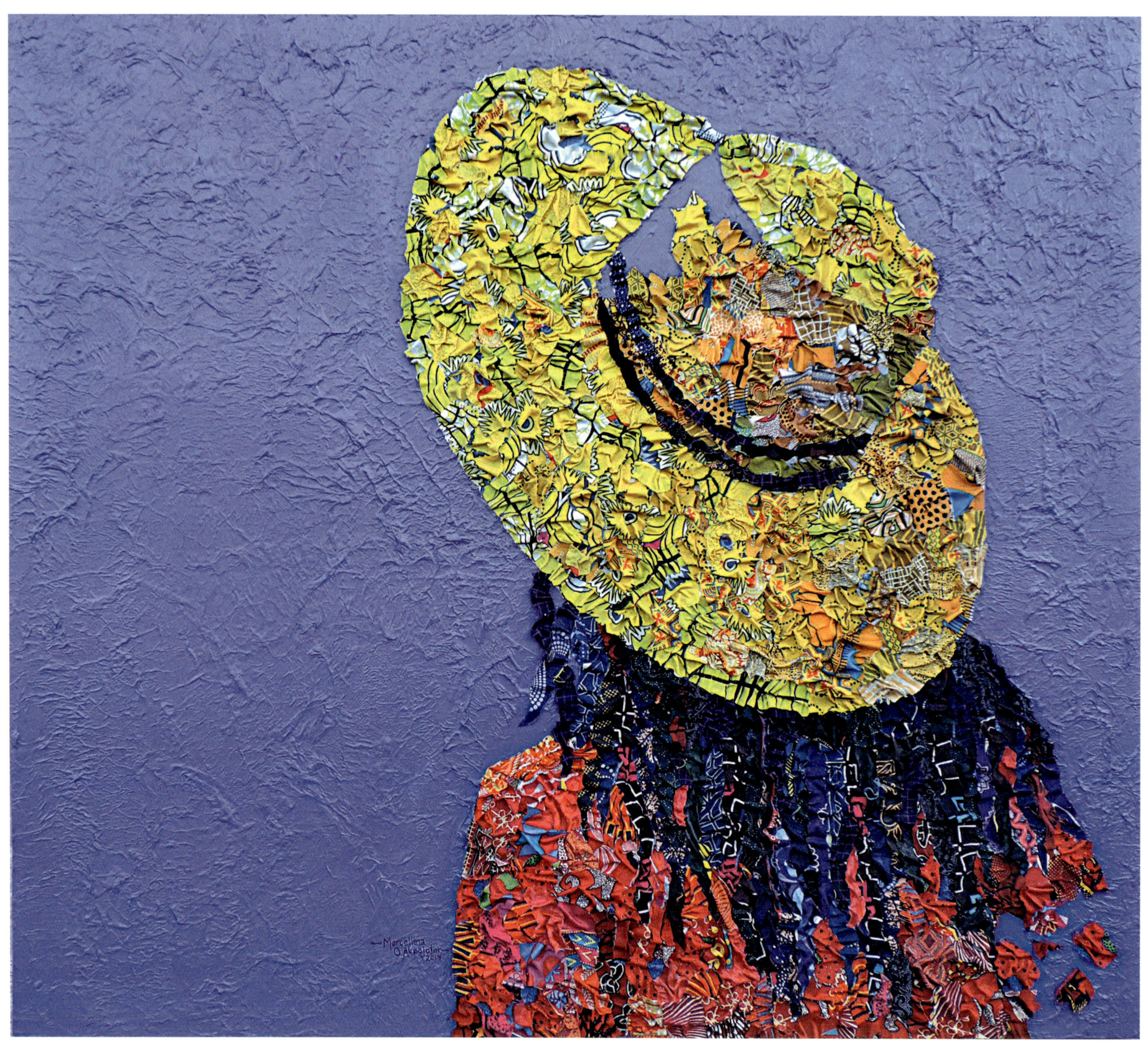

Foreword

Ugochukwu-Smooth C. Nzewi

During a visit to Nigeria in October 2018, I encountered the work of Marcellina Akpojotor for the first time at Rele's old space in Onikan, Lagos. I was enthralled by the body of work featured in her inaugural show with the gallery, titled *She Was Not Dreaming*. She evinced such artistic maturity that belied the fact that she was at the beginning of her career. It was clear that she had command of a distinct visual language that combines figurative representation and collage tactics – with textile, in this case. *She Was Not Dreaming* debuted the first set of works from the artist's groundbreaking 'Daughters of Esan' series. The series, a monument to motherhood and feminism, set the tone for what has become an incredible journey from Lagos to the global stage and her position as a leading artist of her generation.

In my work with contemporary artists, especially those from Africa, it is quite apparent that they place a lot of emphasis on narrative and dialogue as creative devices, because these enable them to effectively communicate social and cultural experiences that they embody as individuals. Embedded in these social and cultural experiences are ethnic identities, often viewed as constructs but which by and large shape how these artists conceive of their beingness and how they relate to reality. Also embedded in these experiences are their national identity (or identities, for those with multiple nationalities) – colonial legacies that inform how they understand territorial sovereignty and belonging, and ultimately enable a cosmopolitan awareness. This composite consciousness makes them amenable to looking at their reality from a universal perspective.

Akpojotor's densely layered work carries all these sensibilities. We track the ethnography of daily life, codes of visibility, ethics of identity, and narratives of domesticity. 'Daughters of Esan', for example, masterfully chronicles the generational echoes of ambition embodied in the matriarchal line of her family. Unfolding across five generations, the series narrates the indomitable spirit of Eboheide Anare Ikhisemojie, her great-grandmother, born in 1910. Eboheide's unfulfilled aspiration to receive formal education becomes the catalyst that propels subsequent generations to reach varying academic pinnacles. Marcellina's canvases become portals through time, extending an invitation to witness the transformative power of knowledge as it traverses the landscape of her family's story. The artist creates an intimate space and invites viewers to partake in the intimacy of this world of her own making.

'Conversation', a 2019 series, addresses gender equality and women's empowerment. Akpojotor takes a nuanced position on the subject, working with a range of media, including fabric, acrylic and charcoal. She creates scenes of communal exchange that invite the participation of the viewer. Each piece signals a call to action to create a future of equal partnership and shunned patriarchy. The overarching theme of this monograph is one of power – power derived not from coercion or repression but from the pursuit of knowledge. This holds true for 'Joy of More Worlds', 'Kesiena's Diary', 'Ode to Beautiful Memories' and other corpora of works captured in this monograph. Her figurative approach is diaristic and serialises aspects of her life into a compelling montage of being a woman in Nigeria and of being a Black woman in the world.

As you flip through the pages of the artist's first monograph, you are invited to bear witness to her remarkable journey so far, a textured history that holds so much promise but is still in the making. This monograph is an open invitation to explore, appreciate and celebrate the enduring power of storytelling through the remarkable lens of Marcellina Akpojotor's art.

Yellow I, 2017, mixed media, 37 × 42 in.

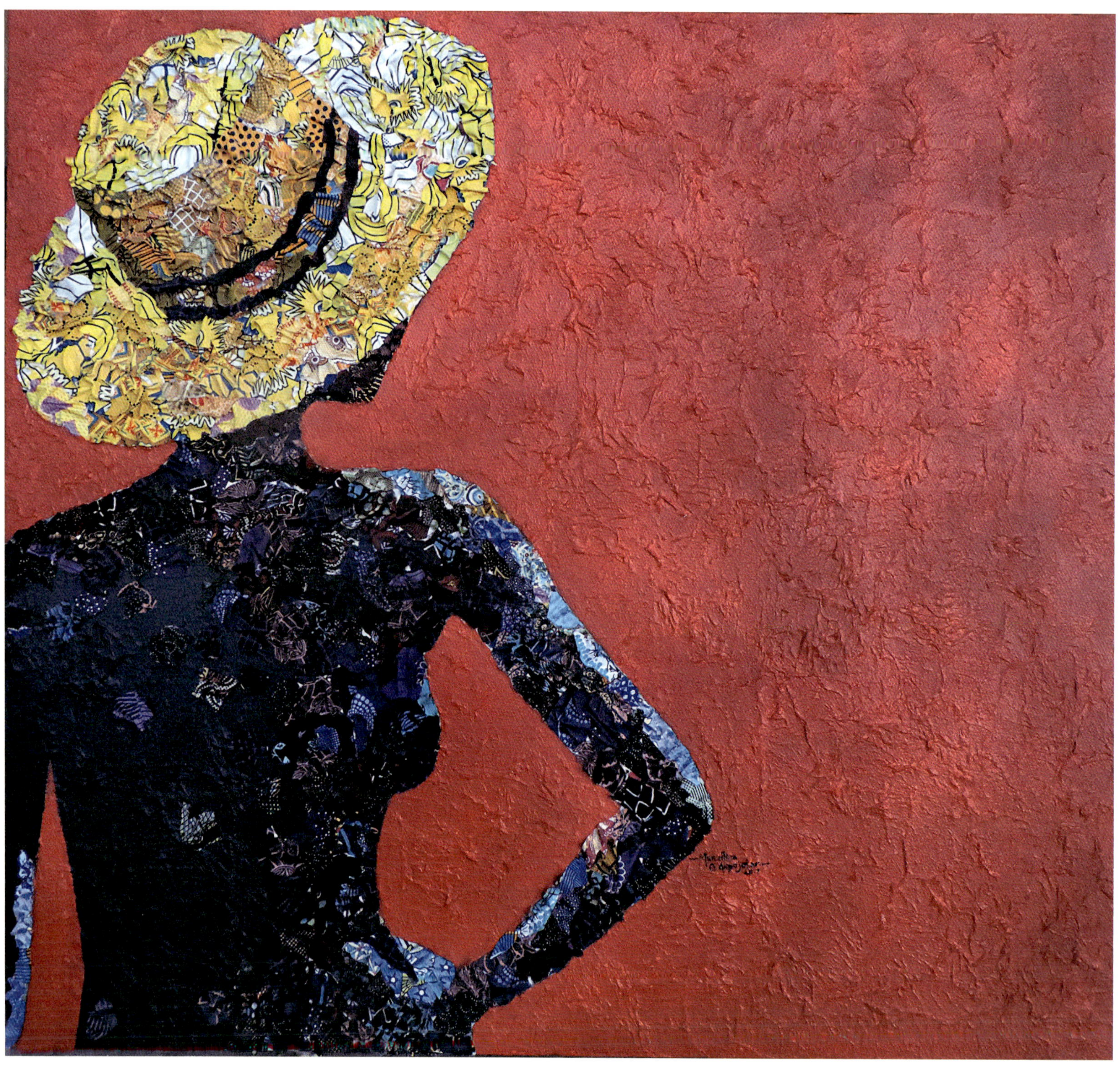

Words from a Legend: Bruce Onobrakpeya on Marcellina Akpojotor

Bruce Onobrakpeya

ON ARTISTIC DEVELOPMENT

It is a source of pride to us from many directions to see how much Marcellina Akpojotor's artistic practice has developed. She first came in as an intern during her industrial attachment days and she did very well. During that time she also had the opportunity to enjoy one of the singular things that we offer, which is the Harmattan Workshop, an initiative created by me to provide a space for artists to grow. She had the opportunity to visit Agbara-Otor, and I think that meant a lot in her development because most times, it is not enough to just attend the school. Many times what you learn from the academy has to be added to by what you learn outside, either through workshops, symposiums, residencies or exhibitions. Being with us gave Marcellina the opportunity to attend the Harmattan Workshop, and that was something that quickened her development. After her training at Agbara-Otor, any doubt about whether she was going to pursue art left her mind completely. She made up her mind to become an artist, and from then on, the growth became rapid.

ON MATERIALITY

Being part of a pioneering generation that infused Western education and skill with more Indigenous practices and materials is something that is reflected in Marcellina's work, particularly in her exploration of the ankara fabric. Our unique environment here encourages creativity with materials, and I know that sometimes people are unable to effectively practice because they do not have the money to buy the necessary materials from abroad. That is not really our issue here. Here, you find materials around you, and what has particularly brought Marcellina to the limelight is that she is able to recycle these materials and use them in her paintings. She got familiar with that before she came to us, and in her practice she was able to elevate it, and that was one of the first things that drew the world's attention. She is a true testament to the fact that being creative with materials is very important. It is also an inspiration for other artists to source materials from the environment. You do not have to depend on imported materials – look at your environment and pick materials that can make you create things that are permanent or temporary.

ON MENTORSHIP

Marcellina was exposed to that freedom of being able to meet a 'master' without the hierarchical distance often found in academic institutions. There is an informal set-up at the Harmattan Workshop that is very important; we bring in knowledgeable experts from different disciplines and the participants learn from them. The difference in learning between this and the formal education set-up is that the informal education set-up banishes fear. There is no master–student relationship that creates fear and inhibits people. I think the learning that you get at the workshop helps augment the academic learning, and by the time all that is put together, you find that the artist is mature, fearless and able to face the risk of developing new ideas and creating new meanings from failed ideas. Marcellina has had the opportunity to benefit from both, and you can see the growth.

ON THE FUTURE

Marcellina has already started very well, and the fear people normally have is that they are not so sure what they are doing as an artist and subsequently get distracted or discouraged from their practice. For Marcellina, I do not have that fear at all. She is working diligently and growing at her own pace. She is also married to an artist, so there is an anchoring, despite the arbitrary nature of the art world.

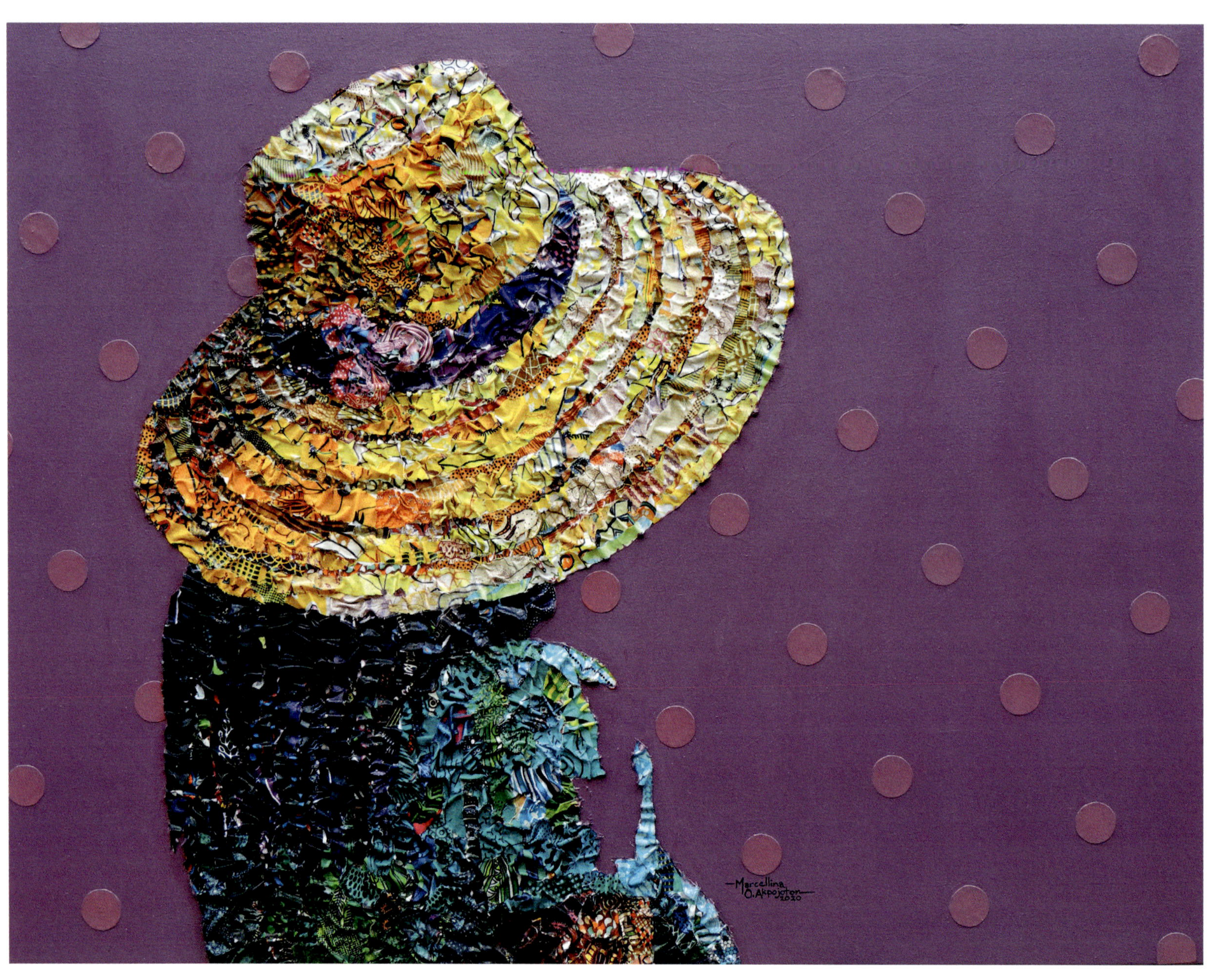
Marcellina
O. Akpoxton
2020

Marcellina Akpojotor: For the Love of Cloth

Marla C. Berns

The Lagos-based gallery Rele opened its Los Angeles satellite space in February 2021 with the exhibition *Orita Meta – Crossroads*. It introduced three emerging Nigerian women artists working in Lagos – Marcellina Akpojotor, Tonia Nneji and Chidinma Nnoli – to a major centre of contemporary art in the US. I was invited by the gallery's visionary founder Adenrele Sonariwo to view this inaugural show under the then-restricted conditions of the pandemic. Contemporary art from Africa was not new to Los Angeles, and established local galleries had been selling out shows of mostly figurative paintings by artists such as Njideka Akunyili Crosby (Nigeria), Otis Kwame Kye Quaicoe (Ghana) and Amoako Boafo (Ghana), among others. I was impressed and moved by Sonariwo's dedication to furthering the careers of these young women artists who were relatively little-known participants in the wave of Black figuration that has swept the continent and the diaspora.[1]

Marcellina Akpojotor's paintings were a particular revelation for me because of her novel use of African-print cloth as a medium. The Fowler Museum at UCLA, where I was Director from 2001 to 2021, had produced a major exhibition and publication in 2017, *African-Print Fashion Now! A Story of Taste, Globalization, and Style*.[2] Research for the project encompassed an overview of contemporary African artists who incorporate representations of African-print in their art because of its ability to communicate post-Independence optimism and its aftermath, as well as key issues of African identity and heritage. These included, among others, Njideka Akunyili Crosby (Nigeria), Peju Alatise (Nigeria), Hassan Hajjaj (Morocco), Omar Victor Diop (Senegal), Eddy Kamuanga Ilunga (Democratic Republic of the Congo) and Lance Raphael Agbodjelou (Benin).[3] Famously, Yinka Shonibare's multimedia installations include figures dressed in African-print tailored to Victorian styles to engage highly political topics of identity and African–European interconnectedness. Akunyili Crosby has been a particular inspiration to Akpojotor, who also uses mixed materials, including acrylic paint, charcoal, pencil and image transfer on paper, to share very personal stories.

RHYTHM OF EVOLVING STORY

Akpojotor's compositions are distinctive from those of the artists listed above in the way she collages actual pieces of cloth on to the painted surfaces of her canvases to depict the actors and 'props' that populate and express her mostly autobiographical narratives. Using this cloth also facilitates connections to history, memory and nostalgia (Cat. p. 52–53, *Rhythm of Evolving Story*, 2020). Akpojotor has taken the integration of African-print cloth, called 'ankara' in Nigeria,[4] to a new level in terms of the fusion of colour, texture and patterning.[5] Ankara has been popular for daily wear since the 1960s and became a powerful marker of African identity despite the fact that it was introduced to Nigeria (and across West and Central Africa) from foreign sources (Britain, Holland and later, China). It was made in Nigerian textile mills until 2015. Akpojotor surely is aware of ankara's high visibility in the public sphere and its ubiquity as a cultural marker in urban settings.

The most common style of everyday dress worn in the mid- to late twentieth century in Lagos was the *ìró* and *bùbá* (wrapper and blouse in the Yoruba language), which has morphed today into more recent fashion-forward styles such as those of international Nigerian runway stars Ituen Bassey and Lisa Folawiyo. Described as an 'agent of change', Folawiyo confesses: '*Ankara*, perhaps Nigeria's most loved and popular fabric, was also my first love [...] we retexturized [it] with intricate beading and embellishment. This one idea was instrumental in changing the way people viewed *ankara*: it added a certain glamour and luxury to what had always been perceived as an everyday fabric.'[6] Choosing to use scraps of ankara, which carry their own memories, speaks to Akpojotor's belief that this cloth is also a perfect medium for telling private family histories – and that fashion can be a potent mirror of culture and society and its refusal to stand still. Akpojotor adapts ankara both in terms of its identity as 'fashion' and as a transformable medium whose widespread recognisability works to recall the past and inspire the future. Hansi Momodu-Gordon writes that 'with every decision to wear an African print, women and men from Africa to Europe, East Asia to the Americas find a voice that speaks of moving forward, being in and of the "now" but at the same time, is ever conscious of the complex interconnectedness of the world, and all that has gone before'.[7]

Akpojotor subverts the flatness of ankara cloth with her method of manipulating and 'retexturising' the discarded scraps and leftovers she sources from neighbourhood tailor shops. By folding, pleating, crumpling and then gluing the cloth pieces to the painted canvas, she adds a highly tactile three-dimensionality to the picture plane. Yet, in so doing, the artist inhibits the legibility of the cloth's own internal design programme and symbolic potentiality and instead transforms it into a personal vehicle for communication.

In *Rhythm of Evolving Story* (Cat. p. 52–53), from the series 'Conversation', Akpojotor depicts a gathering of male and female family or close friends who seem by their relaxed postures to be at home in this intimate setting; one woman stands by watchfully, poised to intervene in the conversation if necessary. The scale of this diptych (96 × 156 in.) makes it feel like you can walk into the painting and join the discussion. The brightly coloured walls and patterned flooring tether the composition and energise the elements created with ankara. All six participants wear different styles of dress that distinguish their gender and generation, and the artist uses the complex textures and swaths of like colours to build their wardrobes and hairstyles, to add subtle details like lipstick colour and nail polish, and most notably to 'paint' their individualised portraits. Having launched this technique in 2013, Akpojotor handles the cloth with stunning virtuosity. Looking closely, areas of faces and arms are left unadorned so that background colours peek through to become painterly highlights. The same signature fabric technique also animates the props of this interior: potted plant, bookshelf with books, furniture and framed drawings. The gallery text accompanying the work explains that the artist 'explores the importance of intimate, layered and continuous dialogue as a tool for driving change and interrogating existing narratives around issues of gender equality and women's empowerment'.[8] Likewise, the painting surface is an equally layered combination of cloth, acrylic paint and graphite that projects the messages Akpojotor has embedded in the visual imagery.

Nothing is gratuitous in this form of biographical storytelling. The framed drawing of a cast brass commemorative head on the left panel is of a Benin queen mother (*iyoba*), most likely representing the early sixteenth-century Iyoba Idia, crowned by her son Oba Esigie. Akpojotor's heritage is Esan, an ethnic group residing in Edo State and related to the Edo of Benin. Formerly kept on royal altars in the palace of the Benin king (*oba*), a head like this refers to the queen mother's importance in the Benin political hierarchy. As the wife of an *oba* who gave birth to his first son and heir, she received her title after he was crowned and played an important advisory role to the *oba*. It is not incidental that Akpojotor draws our attention in this diptych to the power of women in the Benin court.[9]

DAUGHTERS OF ESAN

In her first solo exhibition at Rele in Lagos, *She Was Not Dreaming* (2018), Akpojotor's five-painting series, 'Daughters of Esan' (2018), tells a multi-generational story of her maternal lineage. It starts with her great-grandmother 'Dede' Eboheide Anare Ikhisemojie (1910–1992), whose ancestral roots are Esan, and ends with the artist's young daughter and a hopeful glimpse of the future. The family history Akpojotor wants to tell centres on Eboheide's ambition to be formally educated – to read and to write. The lack of opportunity left each succeeding generation to fulfil Dede's dreams on their own.[10] The paintings present portraits of one relative at a time: Akpojotor's grandmother, her mother and her daughter, along with her own self-portrait (Cat. p. 60). Like *Rhythm of Evolving Story*, the same lushly coloured walls with intersecting patterned floors establish the picture plane for the actors. Each also features repeated elements that have become recognisable parts of Akpojotor's meaning system: seating, a bookshelf with books, a potted plant or flowers, and framed drawings of family members, all rendered in highly manipulated ankara. The deceased great-grandmother Dede is absent physically from *Daughter of Esan* (*First Generation*) (Cat. p. 55) , but is present via her empty rocking chair and framed graphite portrait. The potted cassava plant recalls Dede's economic success, and the bookshelf is a reminder of her unfulfilled ambition to read. Potted plants also serve as symbols of peace in Akpojotor's vocabulary. Every detail has intention and is expressed in ankara, a medium of shared Nigerian history and political independence.

Akpojotor's grandmother in *Daughter of Esan* (*Second Generation*) (Cat. p. 57) sits in a plump lounge chair with her bookshelf at a remove behind her, suggesting that she is a woman with strong links to tradition rather than the pull of modernity. She wears an ankara head tie and what may be the Yoruba *iró* and *bùbá* (wrapper and blouse), linking her to the most popular form of local women's fashion in Lagos. It was not until the early twenty-first century that '*Ankara* metamorphosed from ordinary cloth to extraordinary fashion presence'.[11] *Daughter of Esan* (*Third Generation*) (Cat. p. 59) is her mother, who, Akpojotor shows us in a tight close-up, is seated immediately adjacent to the bookshelf, reading. She is the bridge between the past and the present, formally educated and wearing ankara fashion in a style similar to that of her mother, with blouse, wrapper and head tie, collaged in the same range of blue colours. The clock on the wall may foretell her influence as a role model for her daughter's and granddaughter's futures. Marcellina is the fourth generation (Cat. p. 60), and she is the first to gaze directly out of the picture plane towards viewers as she looks up from reading. She wears youthful contemporary dress with pants and a shirt and her hair is left loose and uncovered. Here, her clothing looks not to be tailored out of ankara but likely to be jeans and a t-shirt with printed designs, including a small Benin queen mother's commemorative head and a royal Benin iron sceptre. Marcellina is the break from the past, but with a clear debt to her mother's influence and support, captured in her framed portrait hung on the wall above her. *Daughter of Esan (Fifth Generation)* (Cat. p. 61) is Akpojotor's toddler daughter, who stands on her own wearing a short chic yellow dress, looking up at a tall bookshelf with a globe. She is the future, with a wide world awaiting her (through formally acquired knowledge and first-hand experience); the angle of her shadow portends her vitality and self-reliance. In the artist's words: 'The piece represents hope that all children will have access to quality education and the world will be a safe place that encourages growth and upholds their rights.'[12]

ODE TO BEAUTIFUL MEMORIES

In *Songs of Home* (Cat. p. 96–97), the 2021 painting in the recent series 'Ode to Beautiful Memories', the artist joins the five generations of women she painted individually in 'Daughters of Esan' into an intimate group portrait. It revisits the importance of 'conversation' in intergenerational bonds and the building of shared memories. Seated comfortably together in a spacious room reminiscent of Marcellina's other interiors, the older women sit on the couch while she and her daughter sit below them on the floor. The absent great-grandmother Dede 'participates' via the altar created to immortalise her. It holds her framed portrait and what may be accoutrements of an Esan spiritual practice (e.g. the double iron bell used formerly for ceremonies). The large and healthy tropical plant may be a metaphor of her thriving legacy. There is no bookshelf in this space, but the successful path to literacy is implied in the open books on the laps of mother and daughter. The cassava leaves painted on the wall refer to the family's economic history. Akpojotor's signature use of ankara to 'paint' her figures reinforces her ongoing commitment to the narrative role of the cloth in her storytelling. The two older women we recognise as Akpojotor's grandmother and mother wear the classic head ties, wrapper skirts and blouses sewn in ankara in a nod to their elderhood and social standing. The patterns in the cloth are no longer uniformly 'folded' and obscured but start to show specific designs. By contrast, the two younger generations wear the shifting styles of fashionable dress in twenty-first-century Lagos. The off-shoulder top Marcellina wears might easily be an original Ituen Bassey design, with her classic use of tailored ankara with tight horizontal strips or loose loops (Ill. 1, p. 17).

Dede continues to be the main subject in 'Ode to Beautiful Memories'. The artist uses an oval frame, which became very popular in the nineteenth century, to hold Dede's bust portrait, *Dede I* (Cat. p. 91). It is worked in highly textured ankara against a lavender-painted background surrounded by a 'frame' of green acrylic paint bursting with collaged, mostly blue cassava leaves cut from pleated strips. Dede's image is featureless and reads as a solid shape created out of dark-brown shades of ankara that typify skin tones in Akpojotor's portraits. A contrasting colourful cassava leaf is deftly interwoven where Dede's face would otherwise be. Her silhouette has her wearing an elaborate head tie typical of her era. In this simplification of imagery and reduction of painted background, Akpojotor creates an especially arresting image that pulses with densely rendered ankara leaves and their symbolic messaging. Next, in another work in the 'Ode to Beautiful Memories' series, *Blooming Red Soil* (Cat. p. 89), Dede's bust portrait fills an oval 'gilded' frame made of ankara that floats freely against its red painted background, which has both stencilled and collaged cassava leaf cuttings. Here, though, Akpojotor creates Dede's framed image out of a complex transfer of cut-up copies of black-and-white and sepia-toned archival photos of her life and times. *Dreams in Bobozi Farm* (*bobozi* means cassava in the Esan language) has an all-over pattern of cassava leaves in green ankara against a red background, which like *Blooming Red Soil* represents the sandy lateritic soil characteristic of the region in which cassava grows well.[13] Layered beneath the leaves are scraps of memory in floating islands of torn paper with burned holes and edges. Many are covered in drawings about education, learning one's ABCs or counting, which invoke Dede's personal 'dreams', gone up in smoke. These new collaged paper elements, like the photo transfers used to represent Dede in *Blooming Red Soil*, suggest the influence of Akunyili Crosby, who uses Xerox transfers of imagery to visualise stories of the past and present. Despite the layers of increasingly abstract symbolism that have changed the spirit and figurative focus of her work, Akpojotor never decentres the power of ankara to offer a robust language of remembrance, gratitude and respect for the women in her life and their legacies. Her mastery of transforming ankara is itself an artistic triumph while also aptly serving her own intention of expressing through it a deeply held commitment to issues of women's empowerment, education, opportunity and innovation.

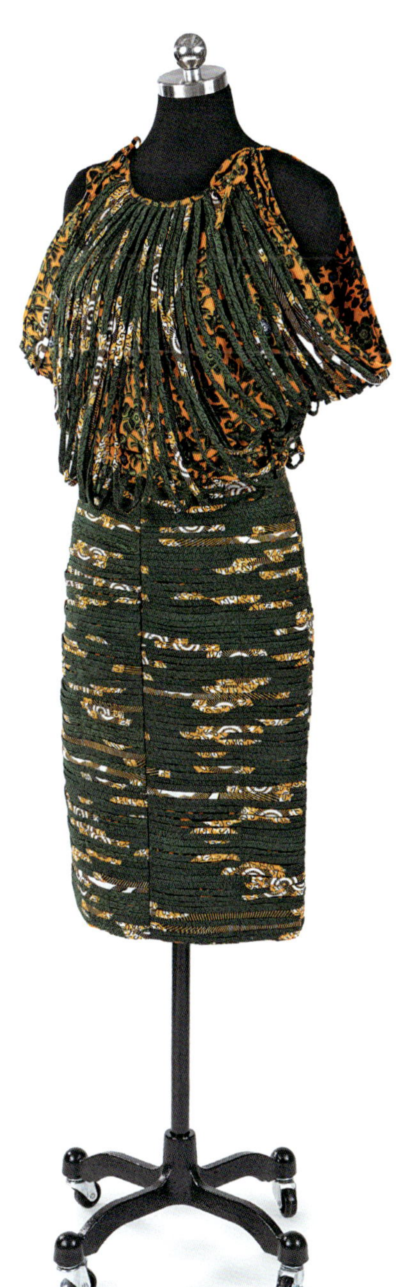

1.   I was asked by Sonariwo to moderate a conversation with the three artists in March 2021 in a program called 'A Global Destination for Art: Rele and Orita Meta – Crossroads', which is archived on the Fowler Museum at UCLA website: https://fowler.ucla.edu/events/a-global-destination-for-art-rele-gallery-and-orita-meta-crossroads/

2.   Suzanne Gott, Kristyne S. Loughran, Betsy D. Quick and Leslie W. Rabine (eds), *African-Print Fashion Now! A Story of Taste, Globalization, and Style* (Los Angeles: Fowler Museum at UCLA, 2017). These same four scholars/specialists were co-curators of the exhibition.

3.   See especially Hansi Momodu-Gordon, 'In the Making: African Print-Fashion and Contemporary Art', in Gott et al., *African Print Fashion Now!*, 263–274.

4.   The word is taken from Accra, the region on the Gold Coast associated with the cloth's earliest appearance.

5.   See Elisha P. Renne, 'Ankara Fashions in Nigeria', in Gott et al., *African Print Fashion Now!*, 163–176.

6.   Lisa Folawiyo in Christine Checinska, *Africa Fashion* (London: V&A Publishing, 2022), 130–131.

7.   Momodu-Gordon, 'In the Making', 273.

8.   The brochure accompanying *Orita Meta* at Rele in Los Angeles offers a general introduction and biographies of the three artists in the exhibition, written by the gallery's curator, Adeoluwa Oluwajoba. See page 3.

9.   See Kate Ezra, *Royal Art of Benin: The Perls Collection in the Metropolitan Museum of Art* (New York: the Metropolitan Museum of Art, 1992), 41 (Fig. 20). Also, Paula Ben Amos, *The Art of Benin* (London: John Calman & Cooper, Ltd, 1980), 25 (Fig. 23).

10.   See 2020 online interview with the artist in She Curates: https://www.she-curates.com/interviews/artists/marcellina-akpojotor/

11.   Renne, 'Ankara Fashions,' 169.

12.   Ibid., she-curates.com, see note 10 above.

13.   Edo State is a notable producer of cassava, one of the key subsistence crops in Nigeria. That said, dry sandy soil with high levels of laterite is not fertile for many crops but cassava grows well in Benin, and Nigeria is the world's largest producer of this staple crop. See https://veggiegrow.ng/cassava-farming-in-nigeria/#:~:text=Cassava%20does%20well%20in%20sandy,if%20your%20soil%20is%20fertile

Ituen Bassey,
Uju top, *Edidiong* skirt, 2010,
'Independence' collection,
wax print,
Fowler Museum at UCLA, X2016.29.8A, B;
museum purchase with Fowler Textile
Council funds.

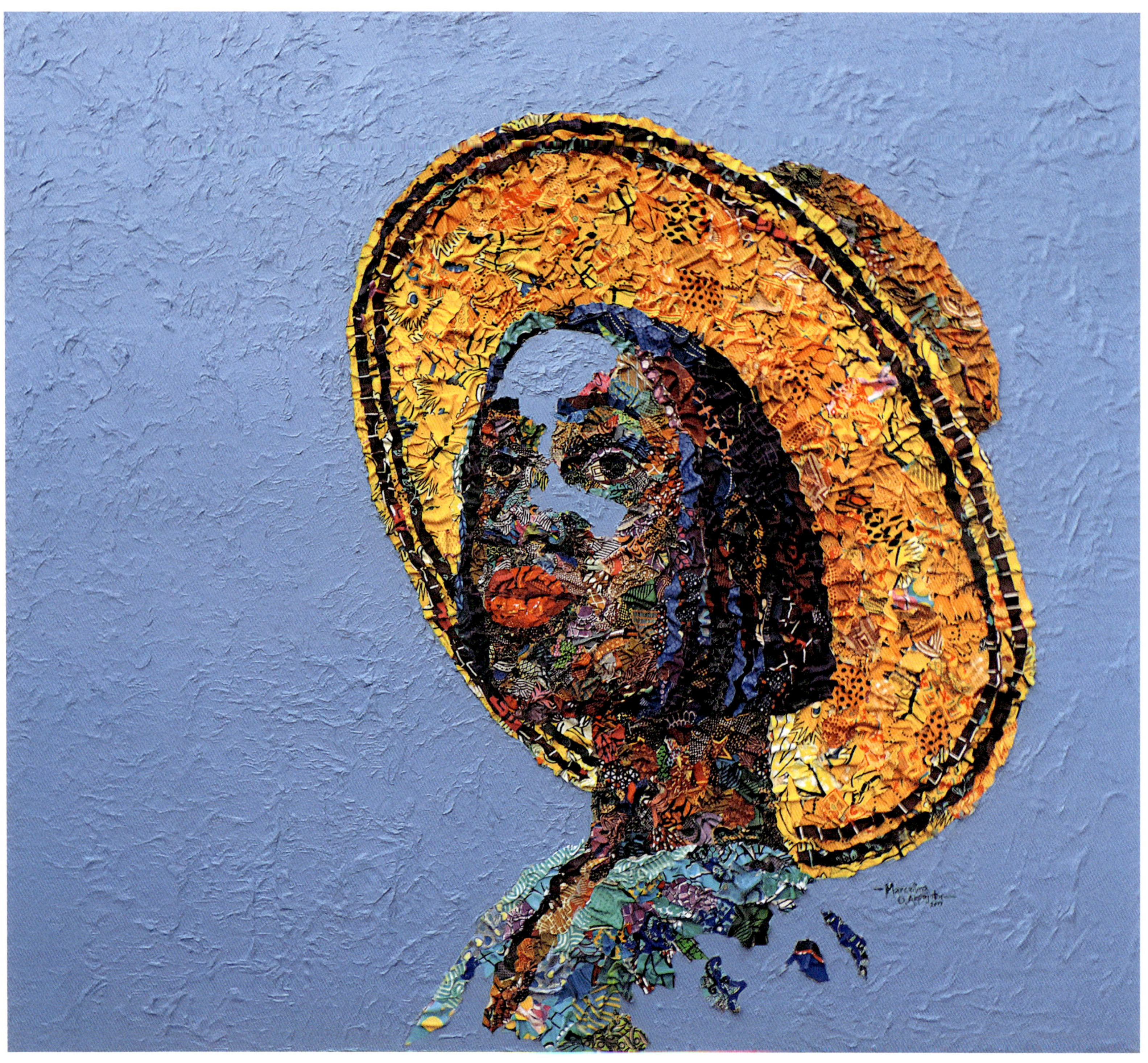

Marcellina Akpojotor's Textile Elegies: The Passion, Texts and Bodily Goings-on

Frank Ugiomoh

INTRODUCTION

It was the month of September 2018 while visiting Rele in Lagos that I walked into Marcellina Akpojotor's exhibition entitled *She Was Not Dreaming*. Her medium, a mixed media approach, encompasses flat colours where bits of textiles and patterns give way to intriguing tapestries of twitchy and alluring tactile surfaces. I was delighted by the body of work accredited to her. I took the time to read the accompanying narratives on each piece. Her family history is woven in threads that provide glimpses of the dramatic personas in her family lineage – like her great-grandmother, Dede, an embodiment of the reverence in Marcellina's storyline. The descriptions bring far-flung epochs of family history into extended discourse. The discourse sketches an aesthetic and dialectic of power driven by feminineness and validates a unique way of textiles intersecting with the visual text: laden with passion, it highlights postmodern oppositions to old cultural normativity.

The works reinforce the Latin origin of the word 'to weave' – *texere*, from where the term 'textile' originates, including the etymology for the word 'text'. Hence, Marcellina Akpojotor's work translates as textile elegies to her family tree. In the above context, they demonstrate how bodily goings-on assume form in the visual text with other textual explanations. Consistently, she shows cloth as conveying the authority of cultural ideas, representing and transmitting family history in embodiments of soft materiality. She adroitly demonstrates that textiles can be identified with collective history and identity, by the bodily tones the texts and textiles create. With Marcellina Akpojotor, threads of memory interpolate historical regimes with the myths and realities that frame her background.

THE TEXTS: A READING

'Daughters of Esan' is a five-composition series with feminine subjects engrossed in texts and bookshelves within the confines of a room. The work entitled *Daughter of Esan (First Generation)* (Cat. p. 55) presents a space with a bookshelf and rocking chair. A framed portrait of a female strategically positioned on the wall overlooks the empty rocking chair. The portrait is a reference to the family's matriarch, Dede. It is the only signified object that animates the piece and its untenanted rocking chair. The picture compensates for the absence of the matriarch, who was unlettered. The series thus narrates as it sequesters chronology among the dramatis personas: an absent great-grandmother followed by a grandmother begets a mother whose daughter bore the child. The visual narrative is permeated by an uncanny focus on a bond held together by a feminist ideology that excludes patriarchal values.

The series 'Kesiena's Diary' constitutes another complement of images, numbering nine. Its narrative focus is on the child that the daughter bore. What trammels and snares

"

befall a child growing up in any environment appear dismissed. The child's nurture is culti-
vated in all instances of her presentation. She studies with a mentor or alone, waters flowers, plays along the clothesline, prepares for school with her shoes fitted by another, and
rides a bike in the company of a mature male. A certain contemporaneity pervades this
narrative, which symbolises a compliment to a young family composed of a father, wife and
children – to a household.

The series 'Ode to Beautiful Memories' is dedicated to Dede in nine compositions in
symbolic registers, except in two. These are *Dede's Corner* (Cat. p. 87) and *Songs of Home*
(Cat. p. 96–97). *Dede's Corner* reinforces the identity of *Daughter of Esan (First Generation)*.
The two compositions signify the artist's and family's great matriarch with an obscure identity. That absence is also palpable in *Songs of Home*, which represents a lineal family descent.
Other compositions do not assume identity but present symbolic codes and signs. Accord-
ing to the artist, Dede, despite her fabled appreciation of learning, was a prosperous farmer
of the cassava plant. *Bobozi* is the name for cassava among the Esan people of Edo State. In
this series, the cassava plant leaf stands out as a motif dominating the compositions. It is
embossed, drawn, constructed and represented in the design configuration of the collages.
In some instances, bits of offcuts – pieces of paper or fabric – are utilised.

In this series, the compositions present a design strategy favouring the emphatic
presence of similar or identical characters. It is a practical design strategy in the applied
arts discipline of textile design. In Akpojotor's pieces, these accumulated duplications
reinforce the identity of Dede, intending to ground her memory within the stable notion
of a farmer. The strategy also gives the artist's composition style and personality as she
deploys alternations and replications in her work. Notable genres that employ such a
design strategy (besides textile design), such as jewellery, architecture and ceramics,
encourage deliberate and structured similarities, including the simulation of spatial dy-
namics. The compositions thus epitomise Dede, whose openness and urbane disposition
to life became legendary.

The 'Power' series is an all-female composition that numbers fourteen, bearing
the prototypical style of the artist. The female figures are all in animated, relaxed or
engaged moods in various sitting postures on sofas, chairs, the pavement or the bare
floor, or standing upright or reclining. The attitudes are contemplative or brooding
when not engaged with a book. The compositions where a book is involved number
eight. Curiously, in four of the pieces the artist incorporates an animal of the cat family. The leopard, also known as a panther, is a wild cat that belongs to the class of lions,
jaguars and tigers. These animals represent power. The book codifies information;
hence knowledge is power.

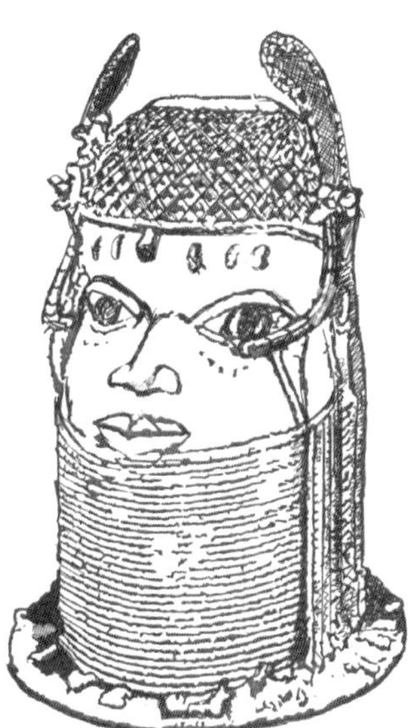

Fig. 1: Late Classical Benin bronze, named *Atolo Ekpen Ha'ae*, with leopard-like characteristics.

Marcellina's ethnic roots come from Esan, which belongs to the Edoid language group. The Edoid languages call the leopard *ekpen*. The *ekpen* constitutes part of the accoutrements of power within the Benin monarchy. One of the diverse bronze heads usually installed on the ancestral altars in the Oba's palace is shown in Fig. 1, a Late Classical style in the evolution of the Benin bronze heads. Its unique name, *Atolo Ekpen Ha'ae*, means that no one messes with the *oba* (as *ekpen*) without repercussions. The *ekpen*'s distinguishing feature on the bronze head consists of two projections emanating from the base of the winged coral crown on either side, terminating close to the upper limits of the coral neck rings known as the *odigba*. Fig. 2, showing a leopard-head hip mask, reinforces the same symbology of power. Marcellina Akpojotor tells us that an encounter with a bronze plaque depicting a girl and a leopard inspired her appropriation of the animal in her compositions as another metaphor for power.

In the 'Power' series, these two symbols of power are used almost evenly in all fourteen compositions. These show either a girl or girls standing or sitting in a relaxed mood reading a book, or relaxing in a book-studded environment with the inscribed image of a leopard. The composition *Quest for Ancient Truth* (Cat. p. 111) combines the act of reading with an encounter with representations of art from the Benin royal court in pages of the book. A balanced representation of the images of power in the series conveys knowledge as a form of power that can be apprehended both intellectually and physically. Education, symbolised in the subjects that are engrossed in reading, enables the narrative to project the ideology of power. By the same token, this ideology acquires authority from the leopard metaphor. In one instance, the artist constructs a vivid account of her great-grandmother's sophisticated life even though she was in fact unlettered and only wished to have accomplished such a feat. The consequences of such a documented history are further extrapolated in other series, engulfing the family tree in the quest to be lettered.

DEDUCTIONS

Marcellina Akpojotor's paintings focus on the legacies that knowledge bequeaths. Pre-eminent is the acquisition of power as accruals of knowledge through self-enlightenment. The quest for knowledge becomes stable signifying markers around her and her family history. A cultured and civilised lifestyle, which education confers, becomes her narrative focus in the family's engagements. The visual narratives, drawn from self-analysis, present uninhibited elegies where bodies exemplify informed values acquired by the obstinate pursuit of cherished aspirations. This longing for learning, as chronicled in the representation of family members, is also a pursuit of enlightenment which is an achievement in itself. Considering that Marcellina Akpojotor's great-grandmother was not literate, a converse signification

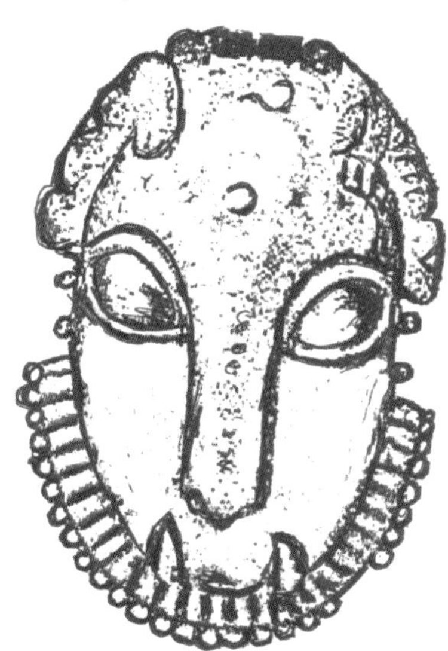

Fig. 2: Leopard-head hip mask, an imagery of power in the Kingdom of Benin.

could be associated with a passionate self-will towards enlightenment through the acquisition of formal education. The above attainment by the family – mainly female subjects –
overwrites the wilful submission to contrived hindrances arising from cultural orthodoxies
that discouraged the education of women in her society.

The factor of power that the narrative encodes is established in the signifiers 'book'
and 'leopard'. These, respectively, symbolise open-mindedness and conservatism extrapolated further. The appropriation of the metaphor of power in the leopard is indexical and
coercive, hence conservative. Its referent is the royal court of the Oba of Benin, where
retribution (one does not mess with the leopard without dire consequences) inhabits the
notion of power. In this sense, power translates as hostile and repressive, an object of inhi-
bition that hinders bodily aspirations towards rewarding social values and statuses. But on
the contrary, Marcellina Akpojotor appreciates that power goes hand in hand with seeking
knowledge and its kernels of truth.

CONSTRUCTING POWER AND THE FEMINIST AESTHETIC WITHIN A POSTMODERN
CONSCIOUSNESS

Marcellina Akpojotor constructs a female-dominated narrative about power with her
great-grandmother leading a family line that terminates with the artist's own offspring. Her
great-grandmother cherished the values of formal learning yet she was not educated in a
formal sense. However, the values she internalised about formal education earned Marcellina Akpojotor's grandmother the right to formal education, which then became the trend
up to her offspring in a trajectory dominated by female characters.

Aside from the acquisition of power through knowledge, Kim Walker[1] notes that
power comes embedded in the stories we tell 'about why things are the way they are'. Thus,
a subject's ability to control or direct the outcomes of a group's social change efforts will
always rely on informed positions. Marcellina Akpojotor's body of work presents a visual
narrative of her family and the allures of formal learning. Departing from the metaphor of
coercive power, she embraces the truth seeker in her unlettered great-grandmother as the
forebear. Thus, the book metaphor becomes the counterpoint to the leopard in the dialec-
tics of power. Within the same dialectic, contemporary culture in Nigeria locates the book
within the metaphor of weakness, where intelligence and relics of falsehood are upheld in
the yahoo citizen's boasts.[2]

Marcellina Akpojotor's understanding and construction of power bear a postmodern
character. 'Postmodern knowledge is not simply an instrument of power,' as Jean-François
Lyotard notes.[3] It refines our sensitivity to differences within a positively cherished culture
against traditional orthodoxies. At least in Marcellina's great-grandmother's era, the wom-

an was spoken for, with less of a priority on her education. But the postmodern ideology allows the artist the cultural authority that is evident in her visual narrative,[4] where she confidently constructs a true feminine aesthetic. The tenor in her visual narratives conforms to the normative liberty or self-determination associated with the self-authorisation that the postmodernist ideology confers, especially where the female subject matters.

Although the postmodern era may appear distant from African cultures, a progressive connection existed in it: it demanded the liberation of the female voice. With postmodernism, the female voice could now speak with deft cultural authority. Postmodernism in the notions of Foucault makes power intangible by removing it from the cultural strongholds that weaken it. The quest for knowledge and truth, where power resides, may appear intangible, yet its potency to reorder society remains high.

CONCLUSION

Marcellina Akpojotor's textile elegies are narratives that address as they project feminine aesthetics of power encoded in the body. That power derives its potency through knowledge as a liberal means to enlightenment. Though women were often held in less privileged cultural positions in the past, the neoliberal world that postmodernism epitomises now allows the actualisation of high cultural ideals.

Following pages
Like Other Days, 2019, detail

1. Kim Walker, 'Questioning Four Types of Power', Arabela Advisors, Greater Good Blog, https://www.arabellaadvisors.com/blog/questioning-four-types-of-power/ [retrieved 20 August 2022]; cf. John Gaventa, *Power after Lukes: A Review of the Literature* (Brighton: Institute of Development Studies, 2003).

2. Frank A. O. Ugiomoh, 'Anatomy of Ageing: Temporality and Transcendence', University of Port Harcourt Valedictory Lecture Series no. 28 (29 January 2024), 24–25.

3. Jean-François Lyotard, *The Postmodern Condition: A Report on Knowledge*, tr. Geoff Bennington and Brian Massumi, foreword by Fredric Jameson (Minneapolis: University of Minnesota Press, 1984).

4. Craig Owens, 'The Discourse of Others: Feminists and Postmodernism' (1983), in Donald Preziosi, ed., *The Art of Art History: A Critical Anthology* (Oxford: Oxford University Press, 2009), 335.

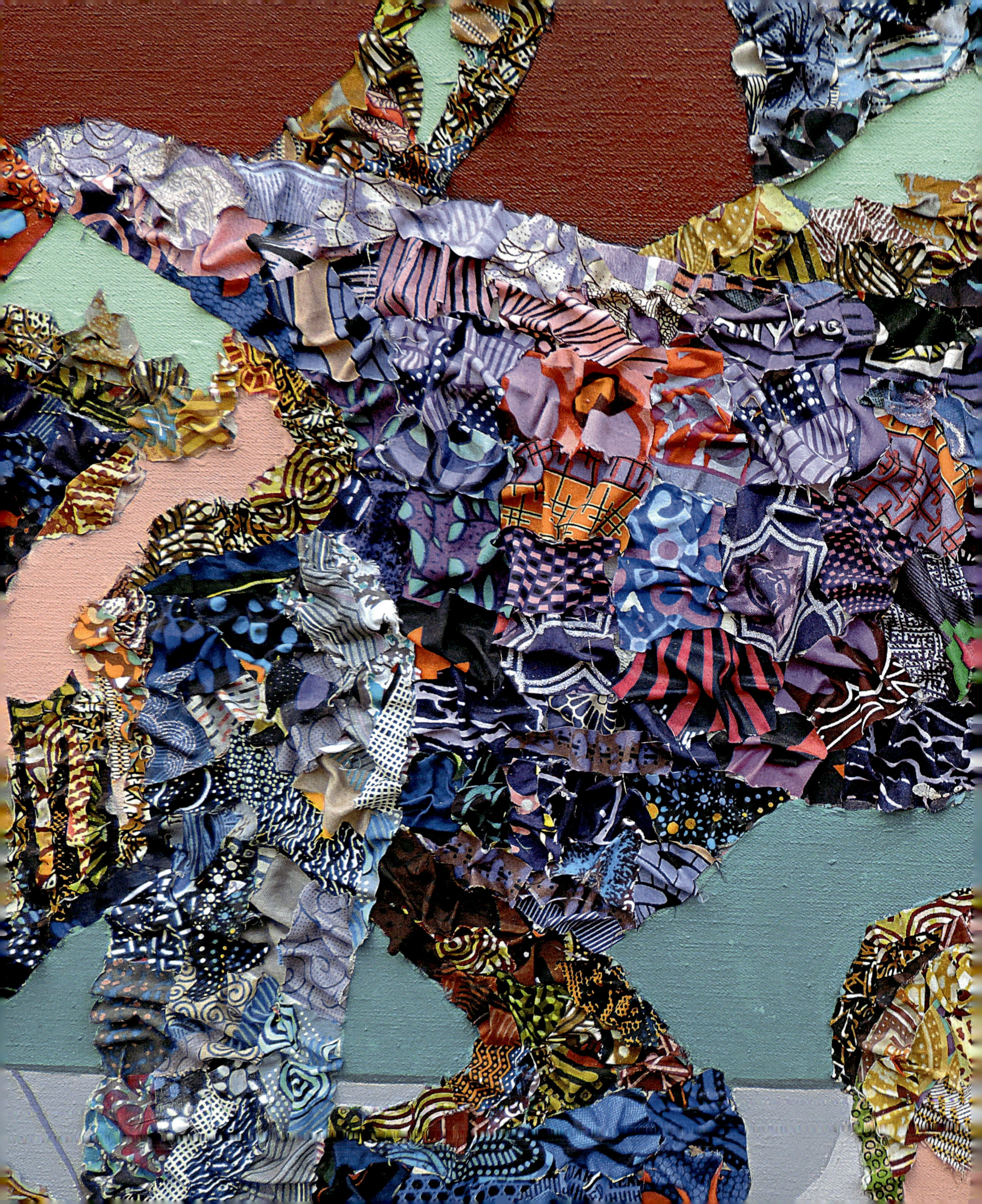

WORKS

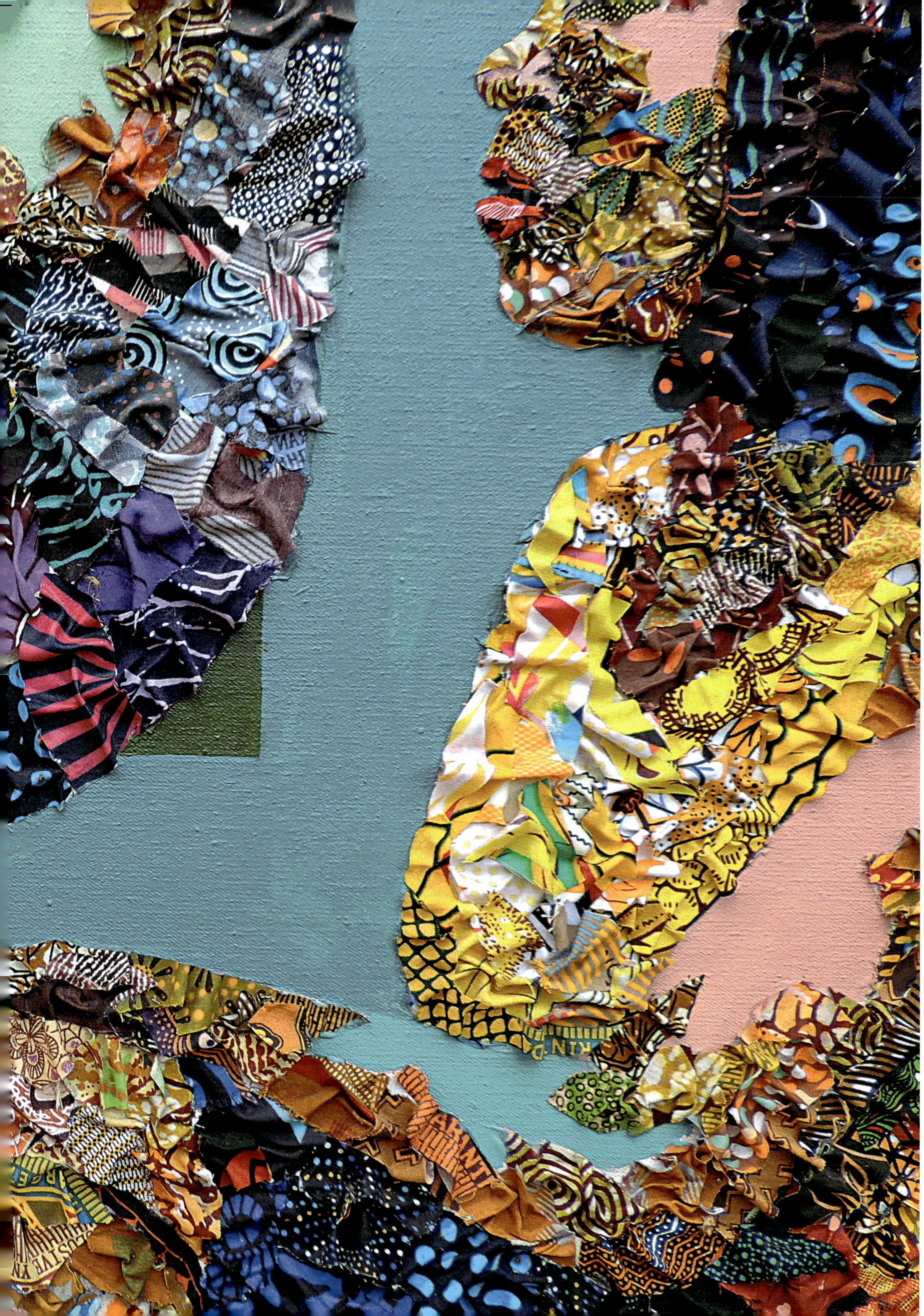

COME WHAT MAY

This series explores the relationship between women and education and the challenges faced in accessing it.

Women have to face their studies while also looking over their shoulders. Some have to study amidst fear, which impacts their academic experience and state of mind.

In some of the works, the figures look away from the book in their hands, holding the gaze of their audience. This stance also means they have a view of their environment.

As they access the opportunity of education they must also as a matter of caution be overly conscious of themselves and their surroundings to ensure they do not fall victim to sexual harassment.

Marcellina Akpojotor was inspired to create this body of work following the premiere of BBC Africa Eye's *Sex for Grades* documentary.

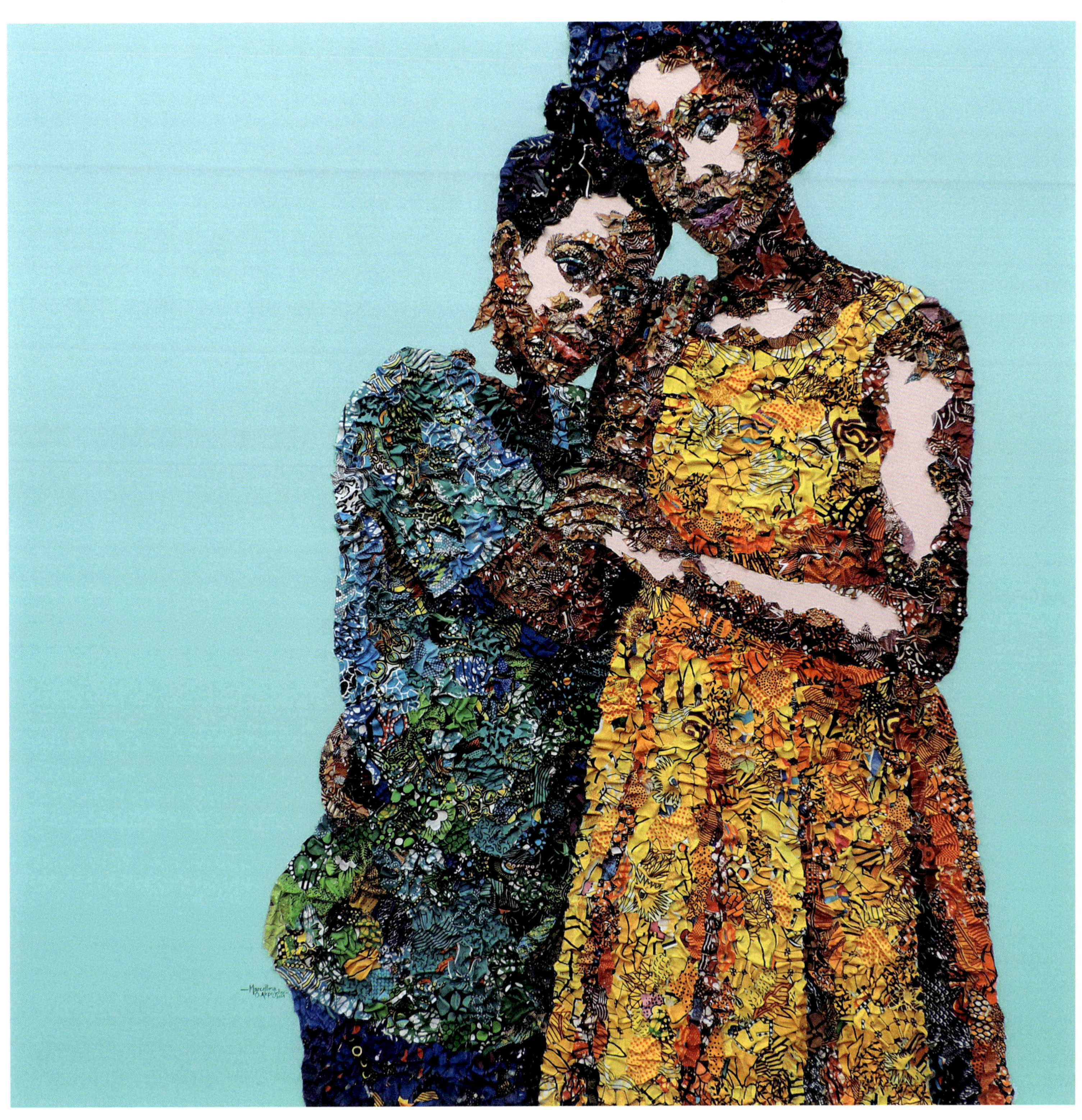

Sister Sister, 2019,
mixed media,
48 × 48 in.

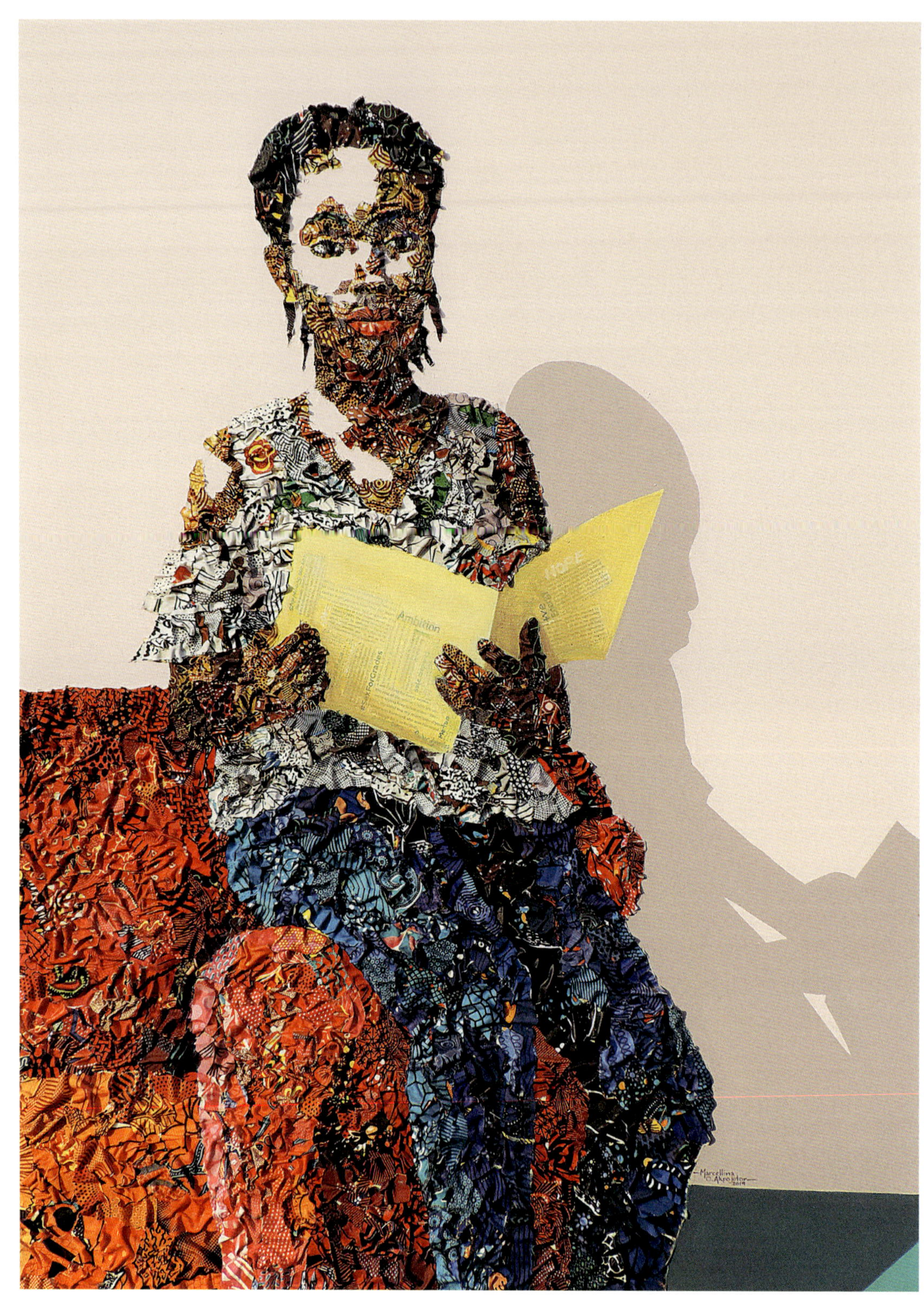

Still I Rise I, 2019,
mixed media,
48 × 36 in.

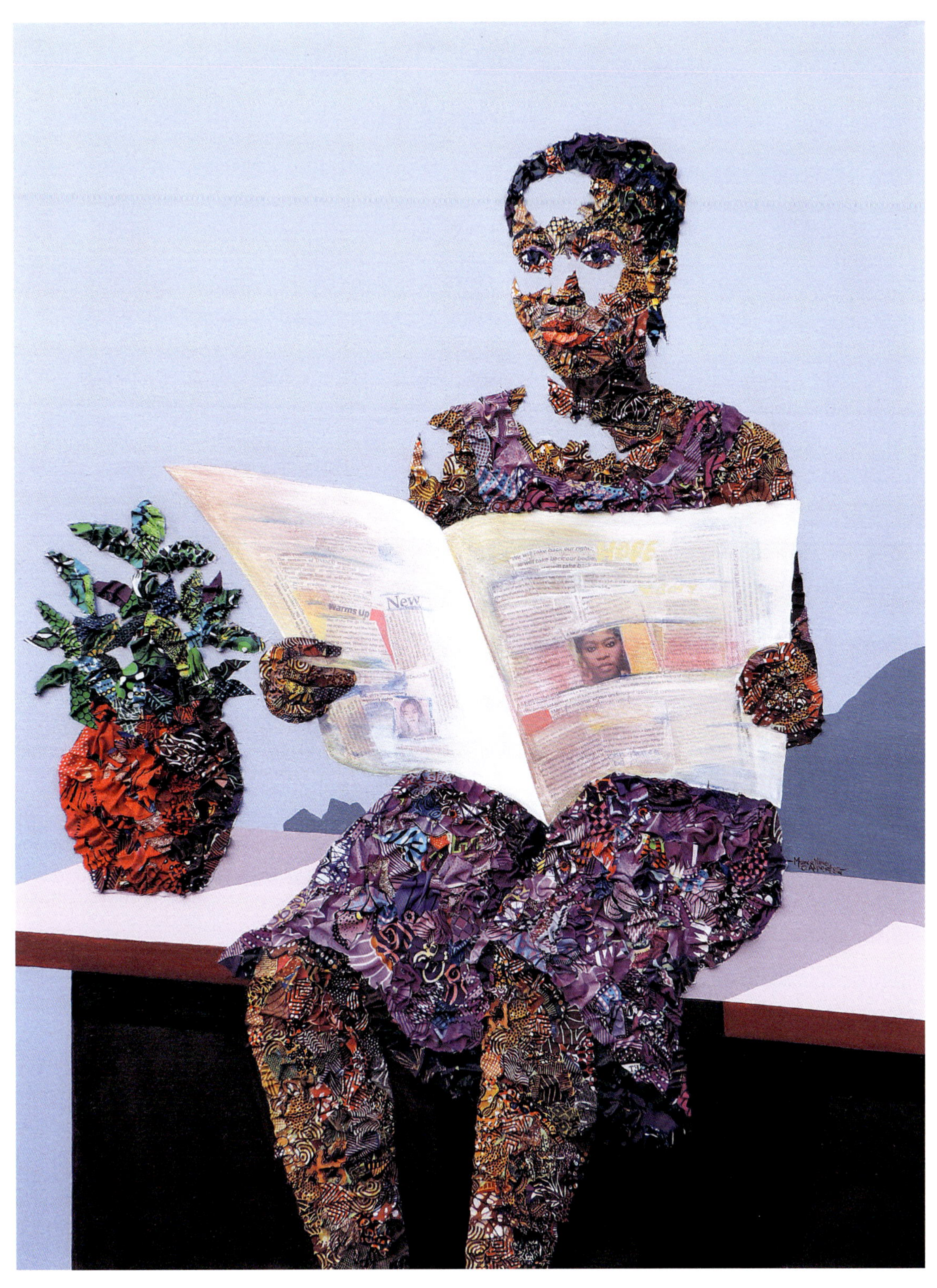

Still I Rise II, 2019,
mixed media,
48 × 36 in.

Yellow Memories, 2019,
mixed media,
40 × 60 in.

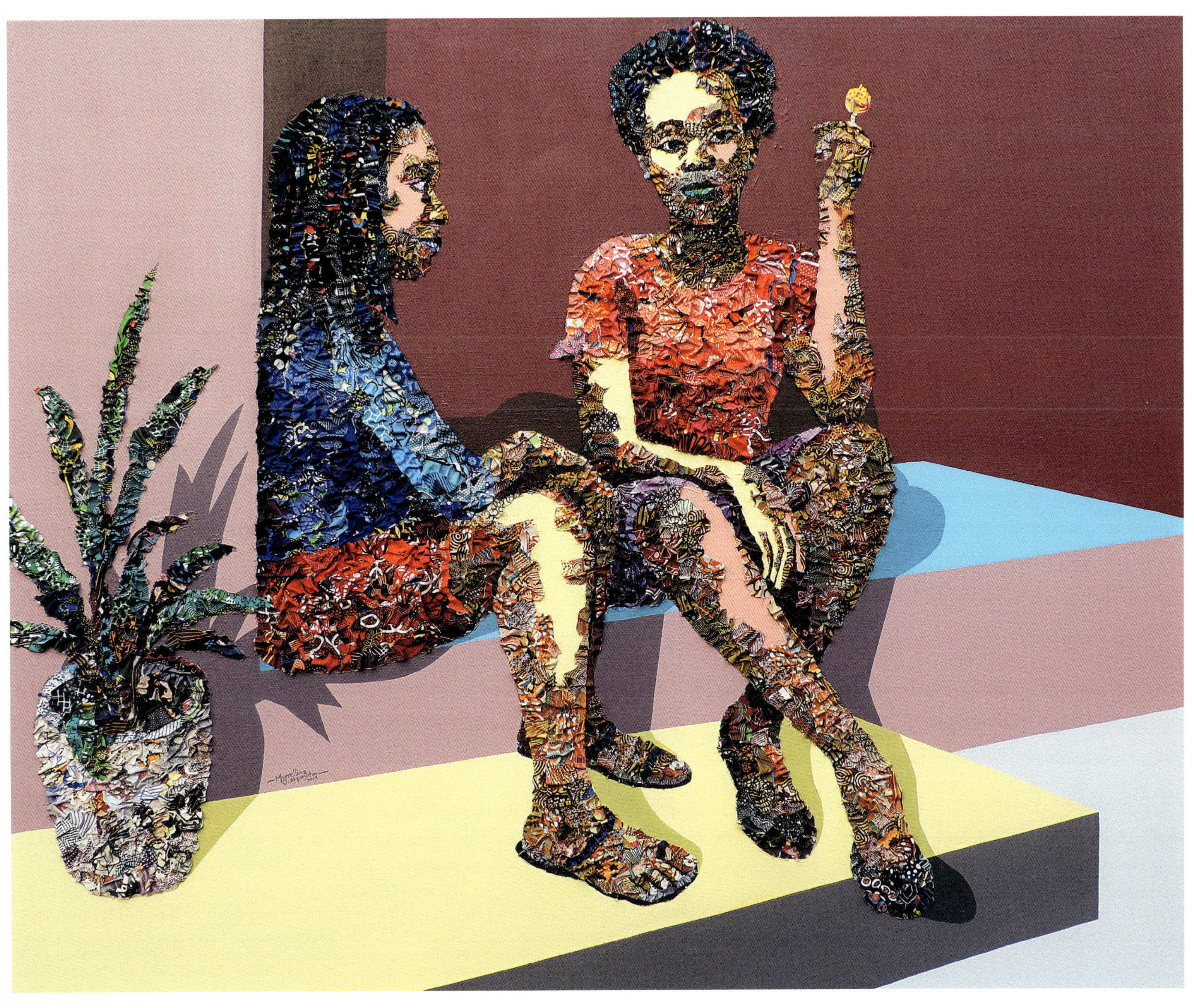

CONVERSATION

In her 'Conversation' series, Marcellina Akpojotor explores the importance of intimate, layered and continuous dialogue as a tool for driving change and interrogating existing narratives, especially around issues on gender equality and women's empowerment.

Working across several media including fabric, acrylic and charcoal, she creates intimate scenes populated with dynamic figures in various positions of repose engaged in communal discourse. With this series, Akpojotor points to a need for constant, critical conversation in shaping and mapping out new futures of gender equality and empowerment devoid of patriarchal oppression and marginalisation.

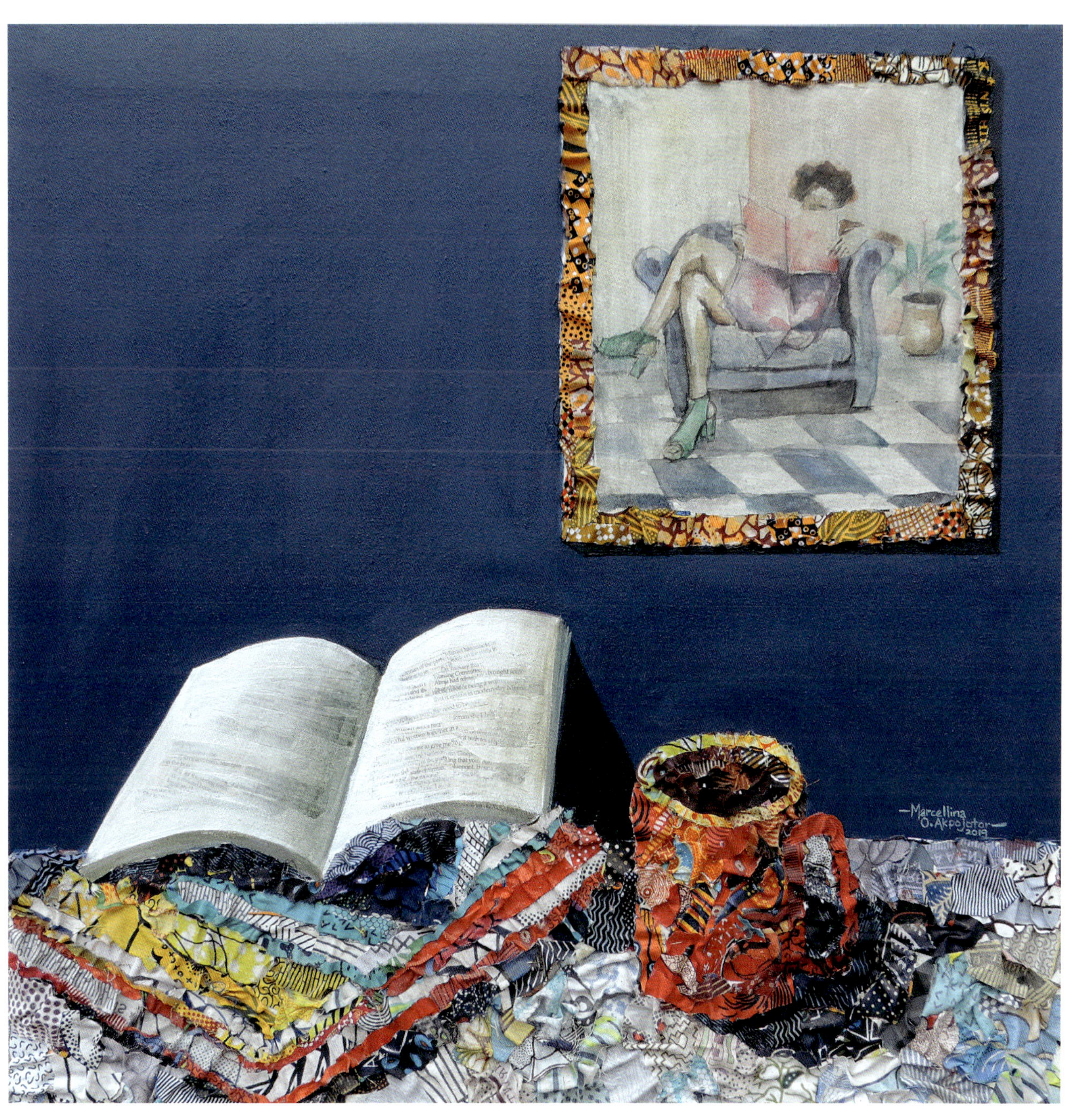

My Cup of Tea, 2019,
mixed media,
24 × 24 in.

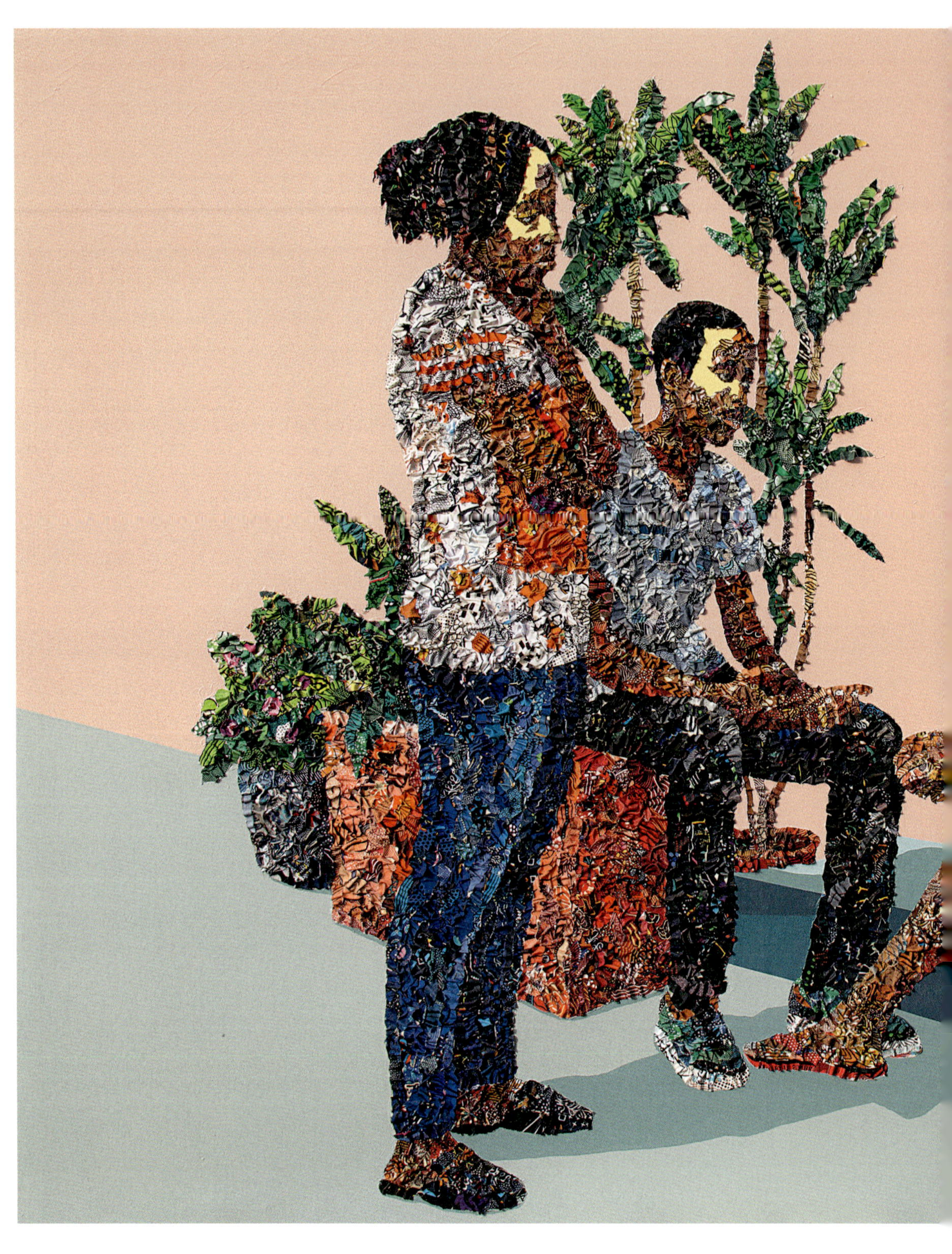

At the Backyard, 2022,
fabric and acrylic on canvas,
60 × 77 in.

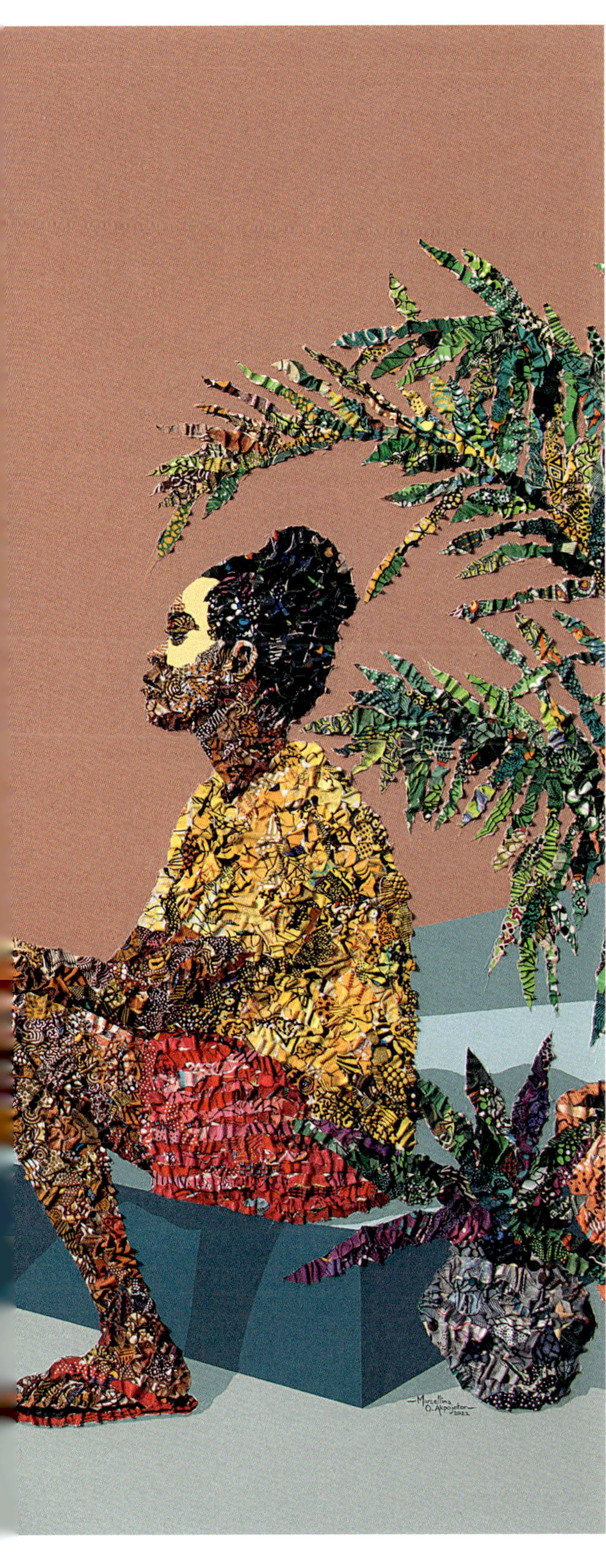

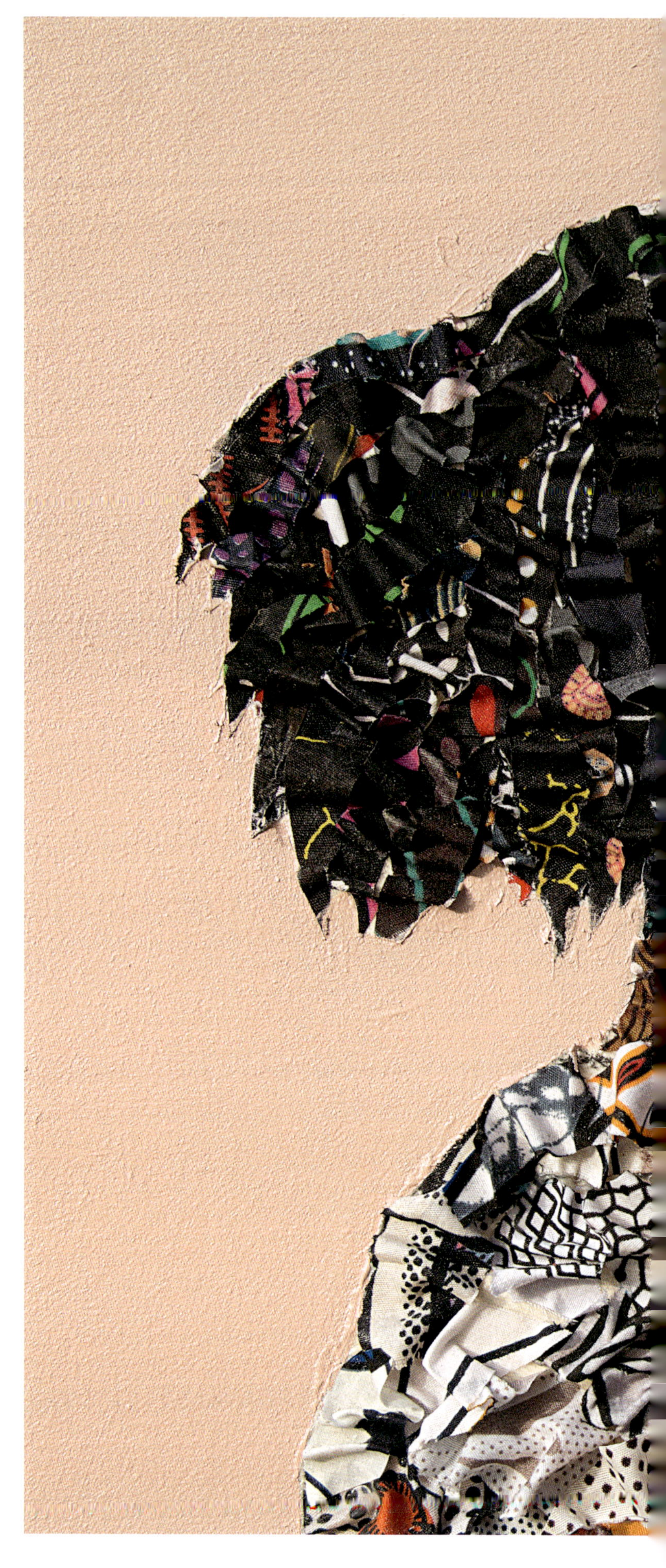

At the Backyard, 2022, detail

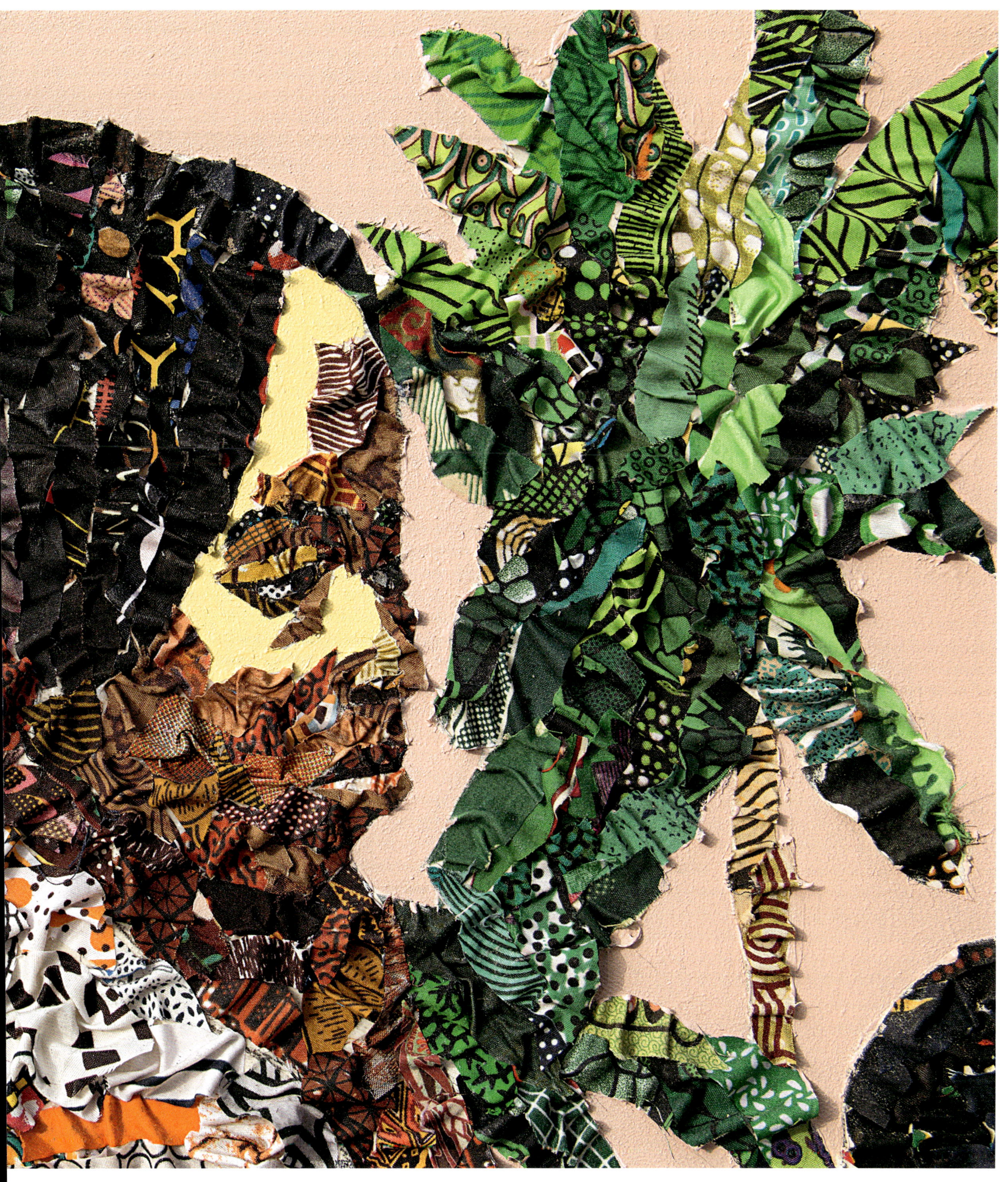

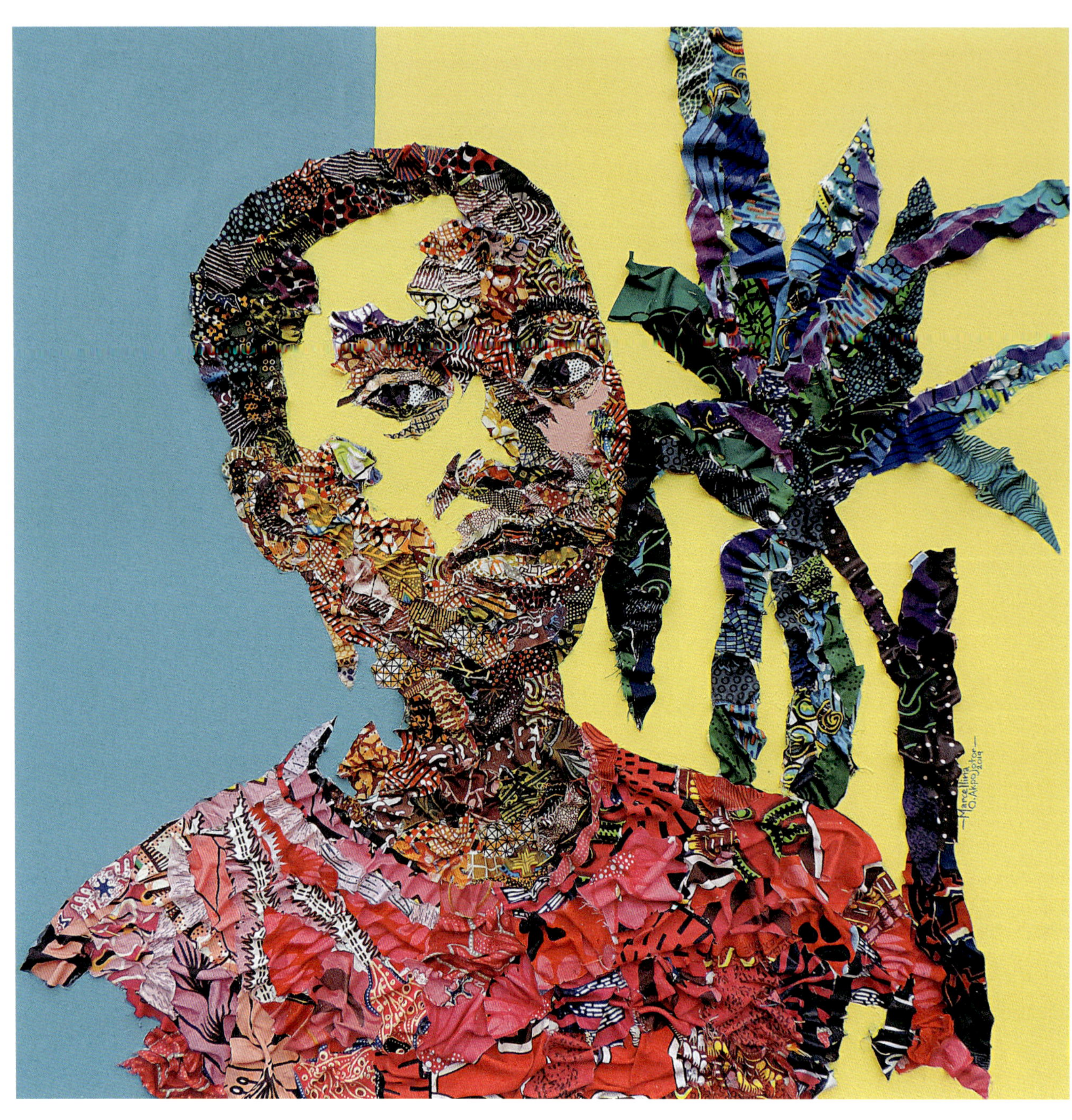

Young One, 2019,
mixed media,
24 × 24 in.

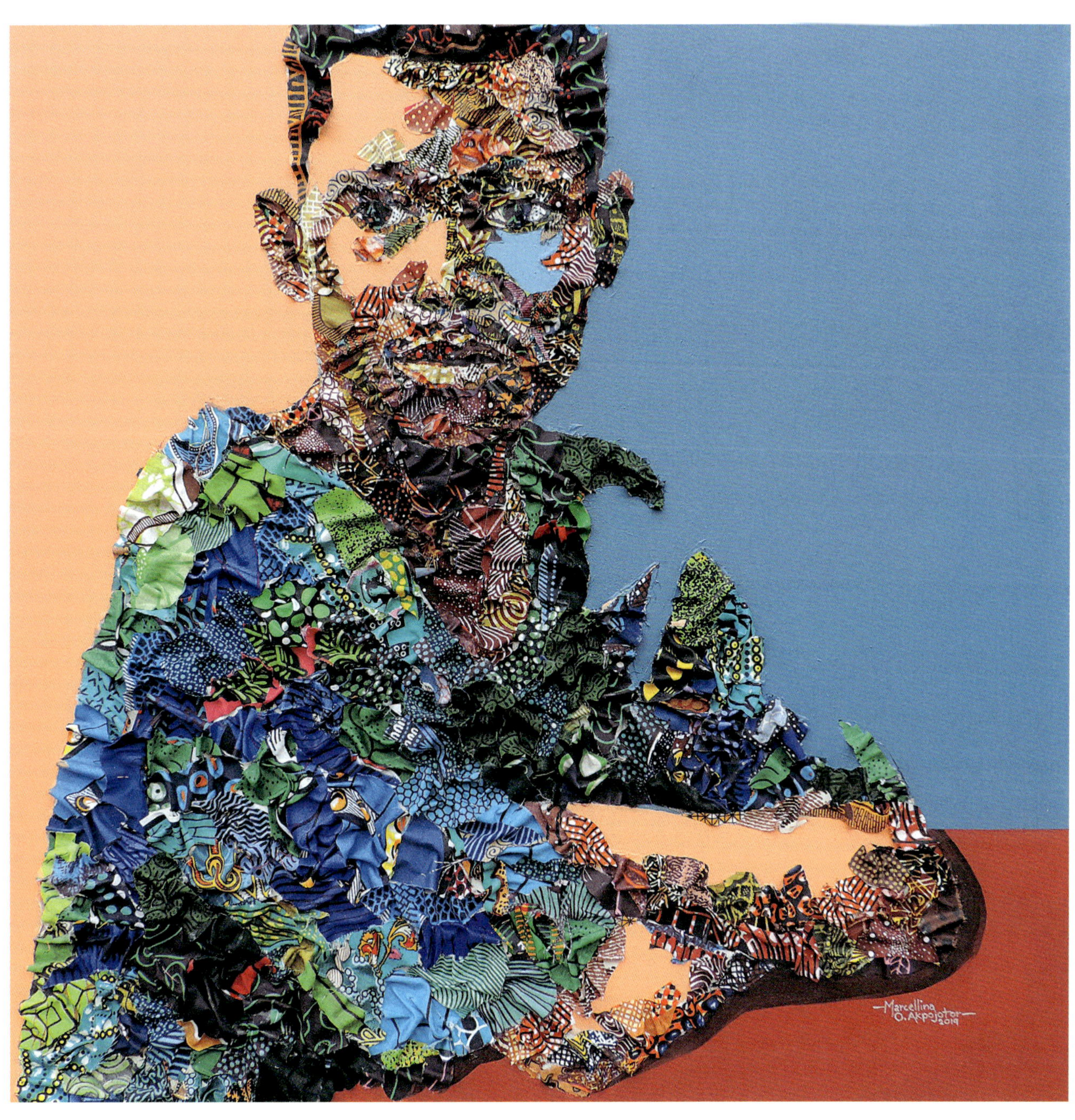

Here for Change, 2019,
mixed media,
24 × 24 in.

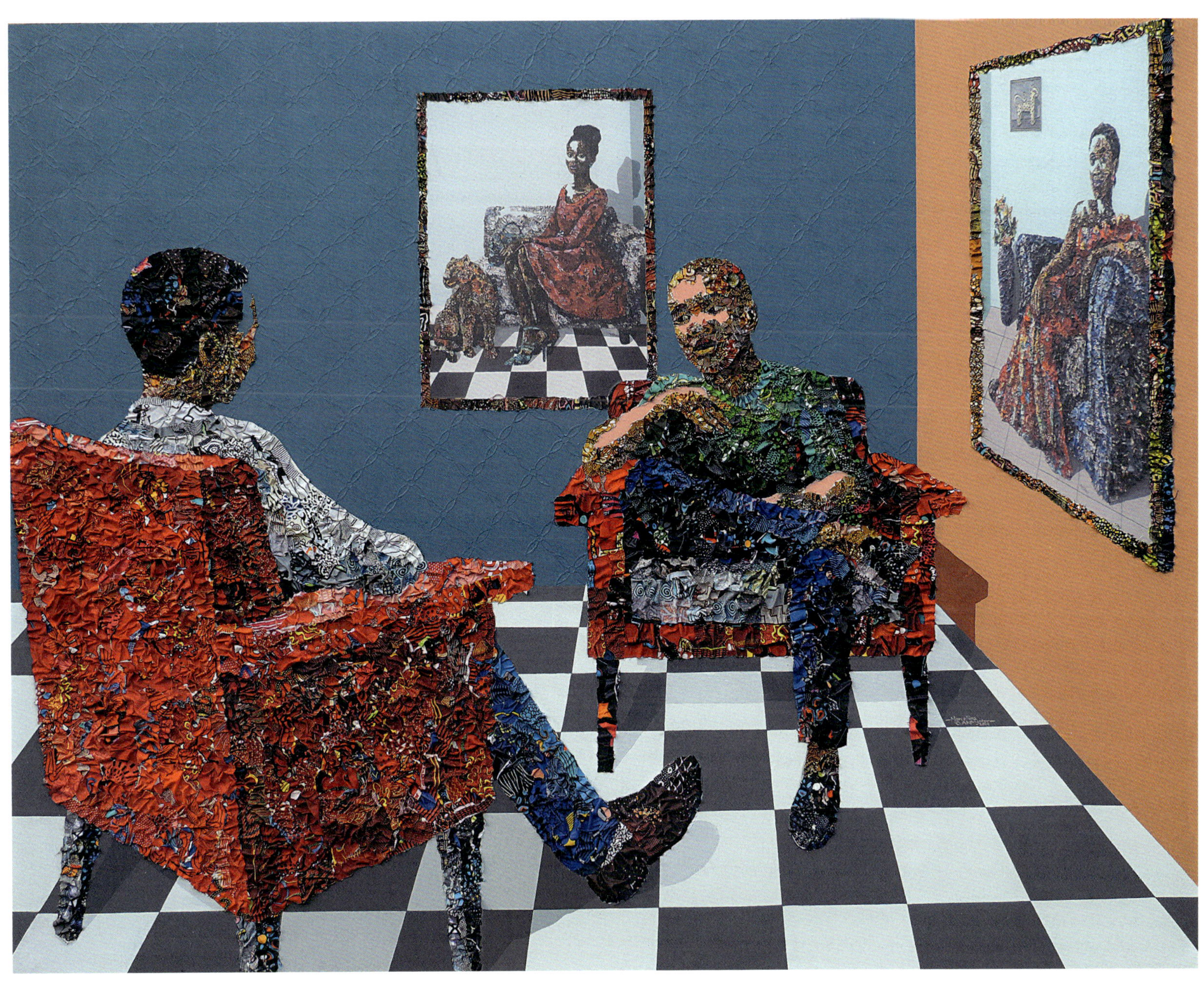

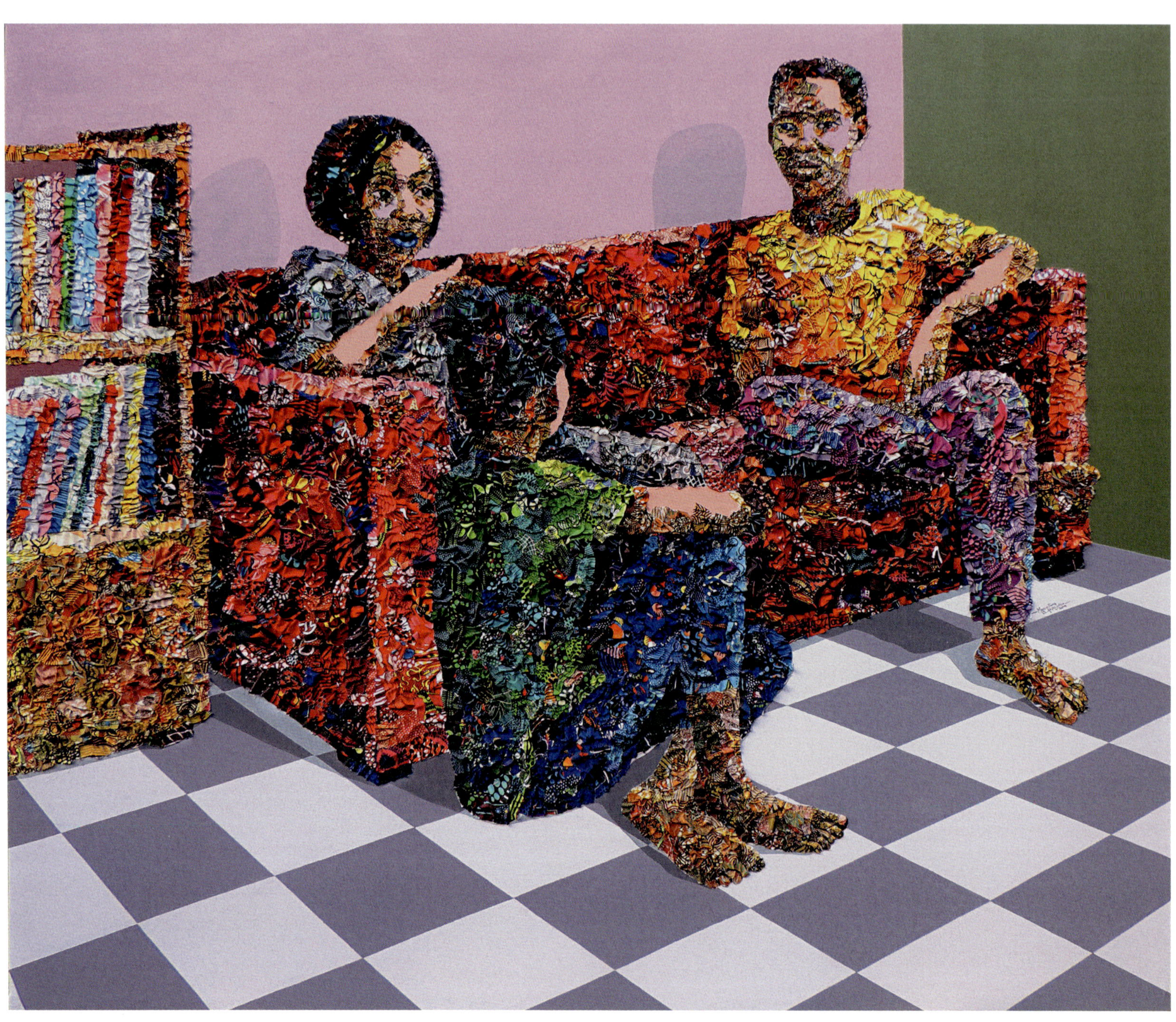

Red Couch Talk, 2019,
mixed media,
60 × 72 in.

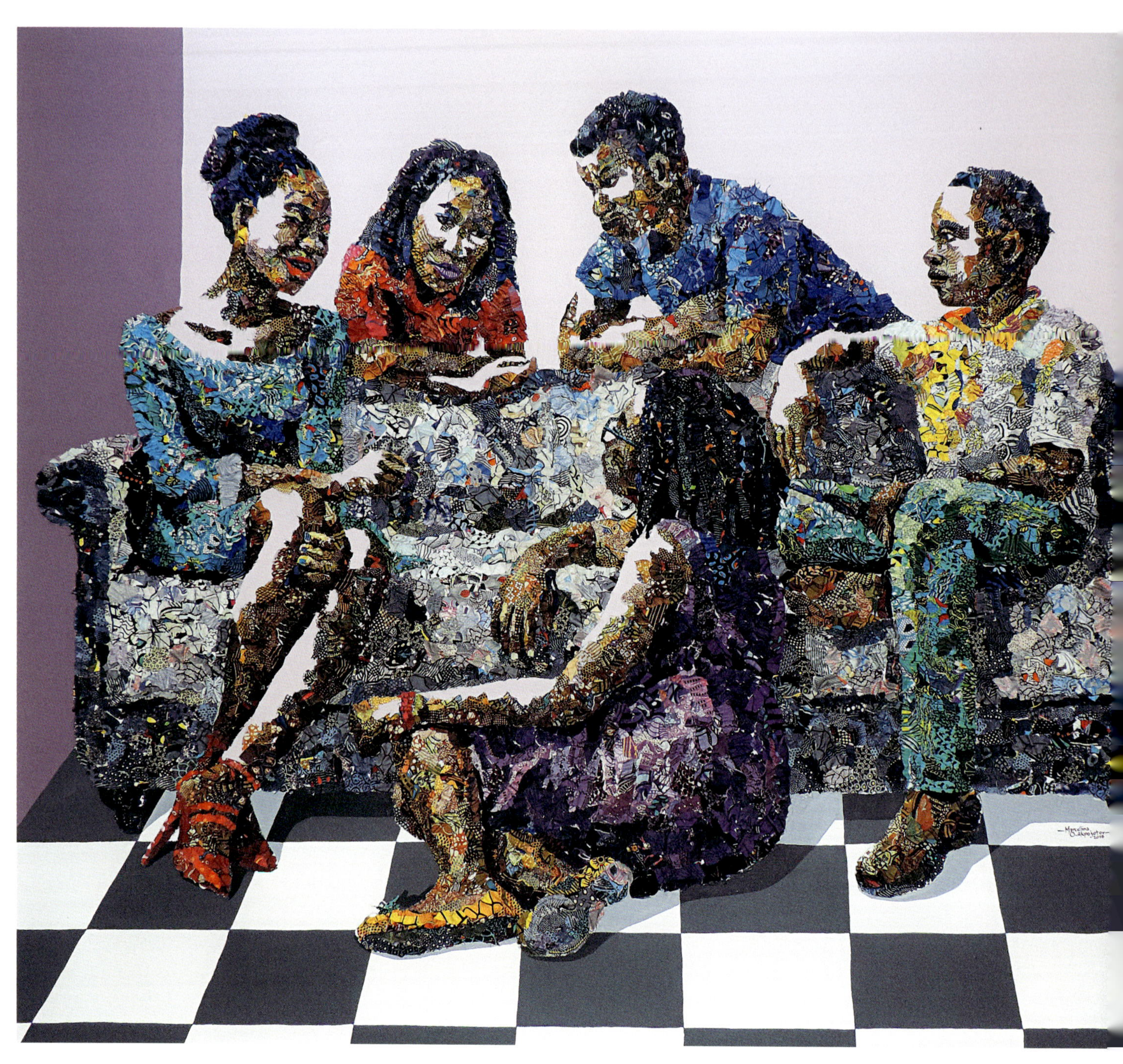

In Conversation ..., 2018,
mixed media,
60 × 84 in.

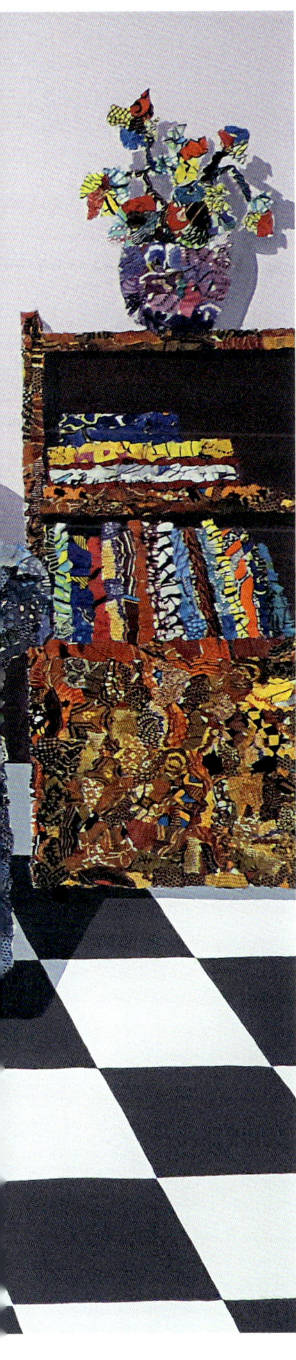

Like Other Days, 2019,
mixed media,
60 × 77 in.

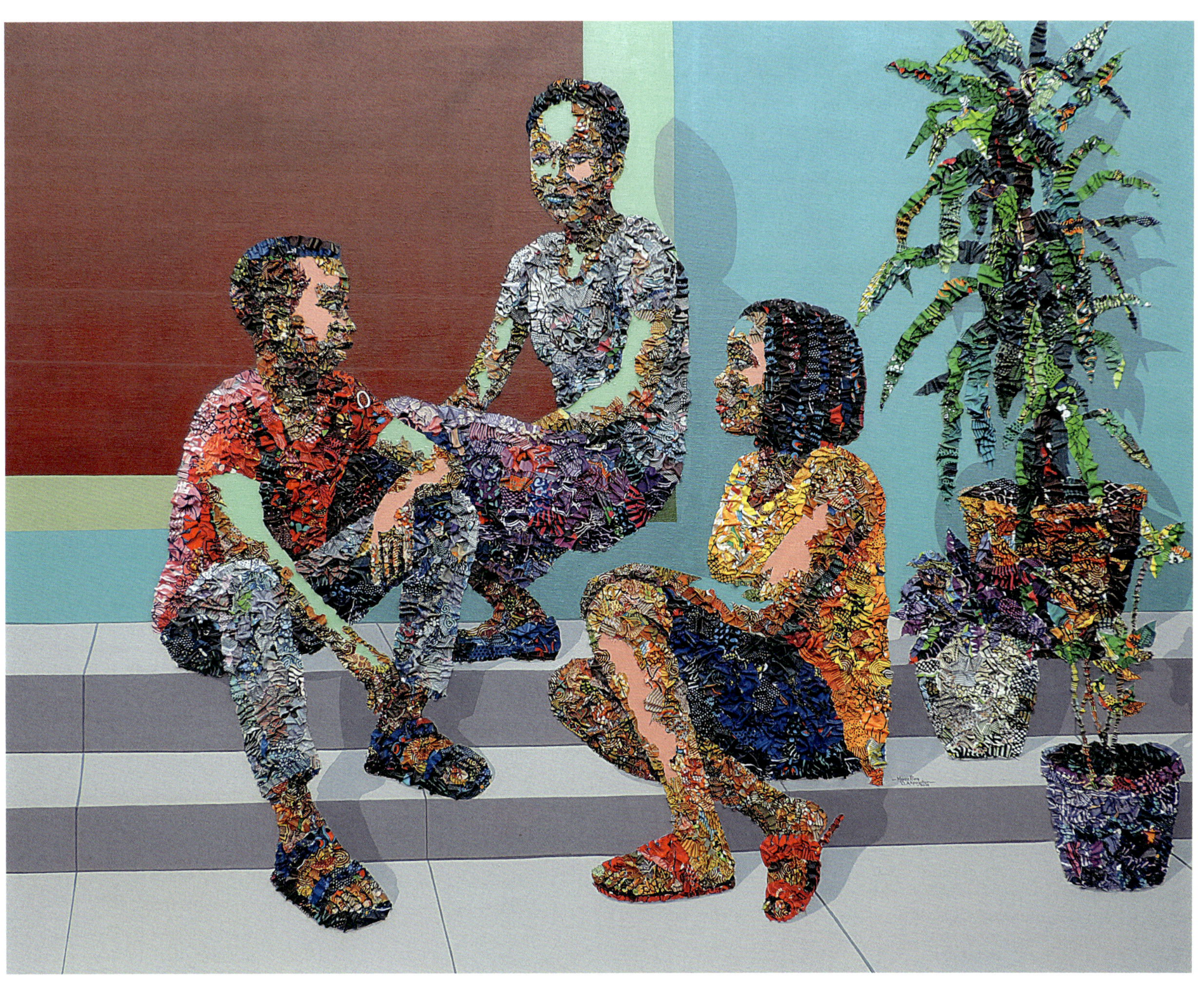

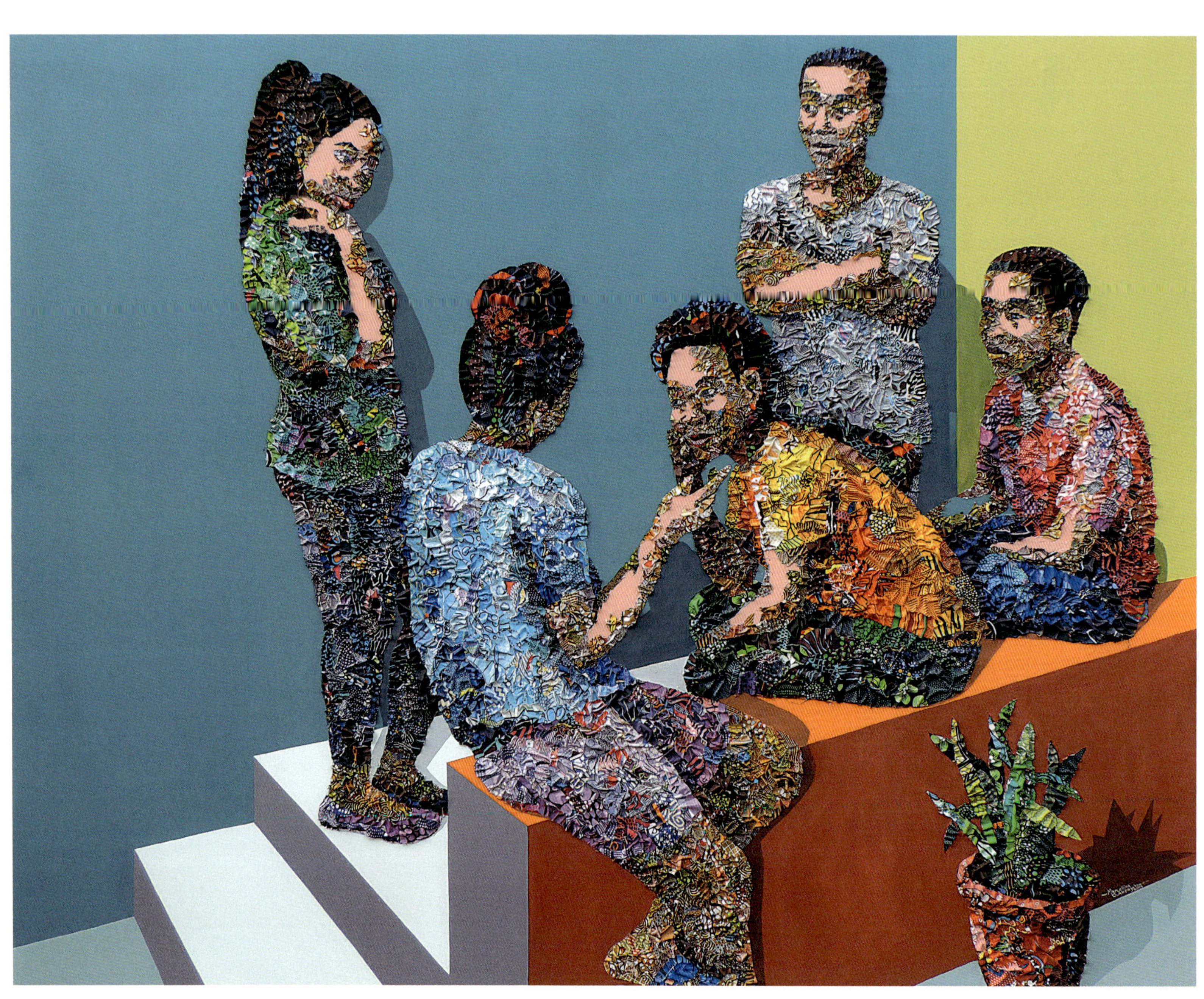

Closing the Gap, 2019,
mixed media,
60 × 77 in.

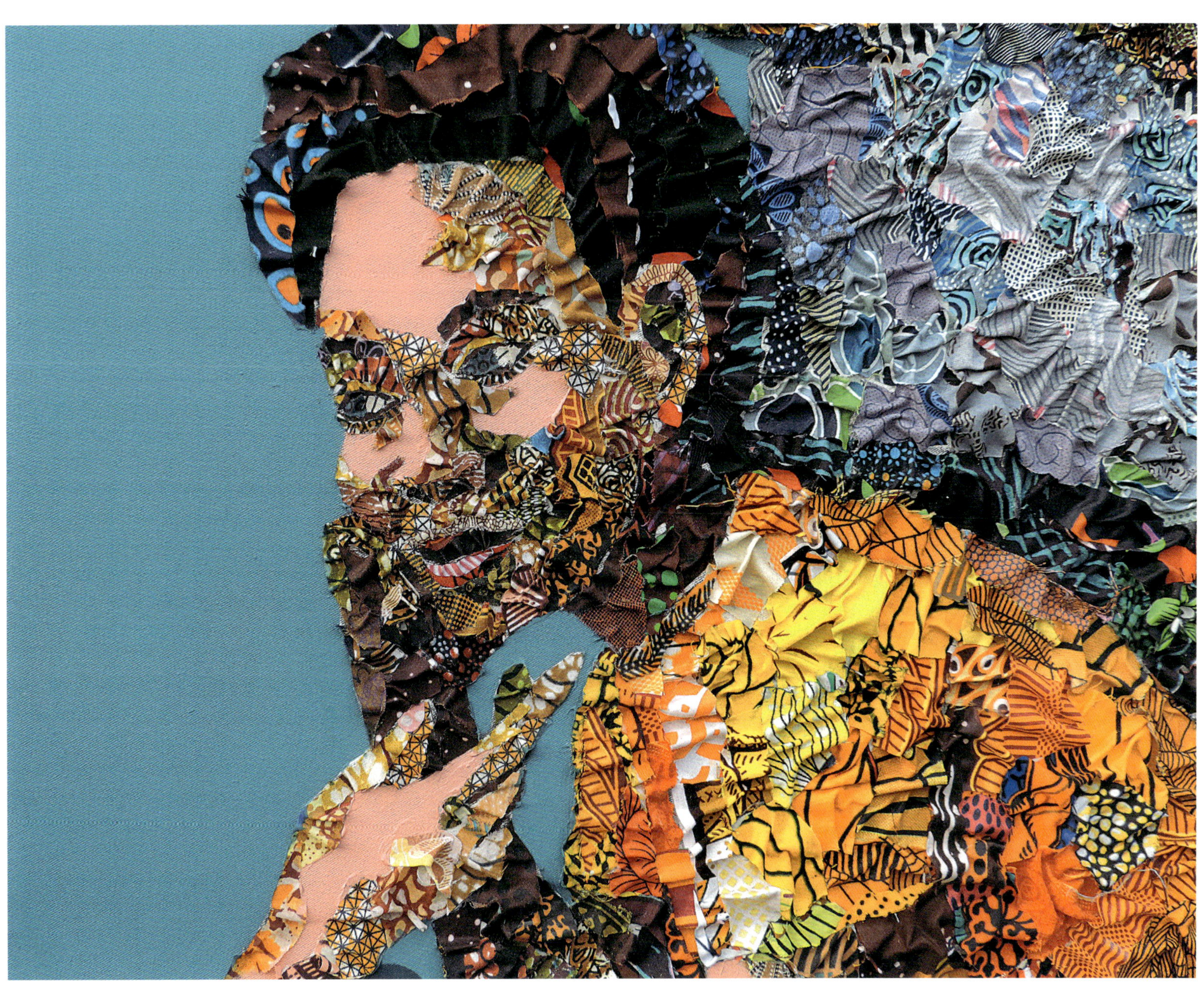

Closing the Gap, 2019, detail

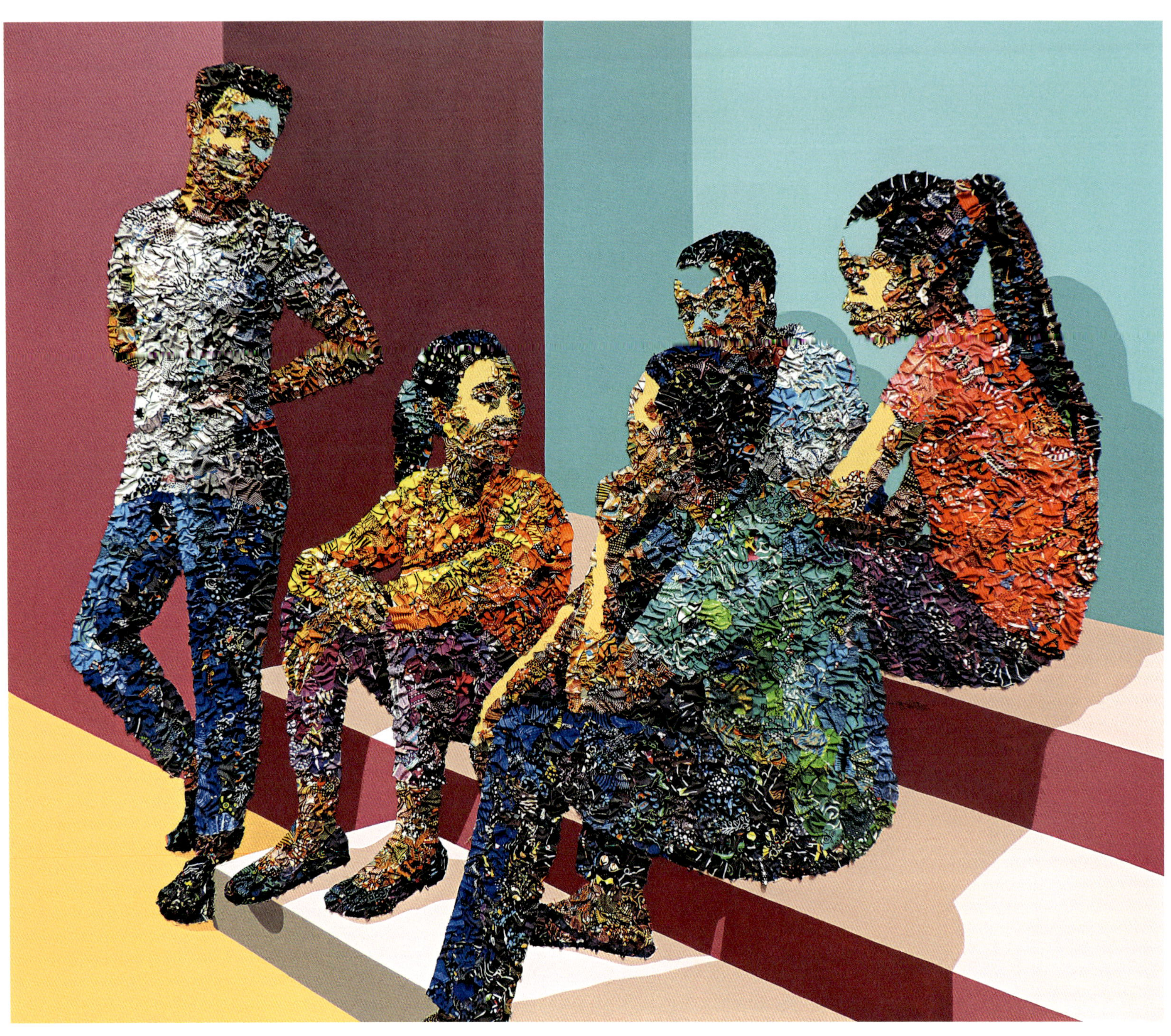

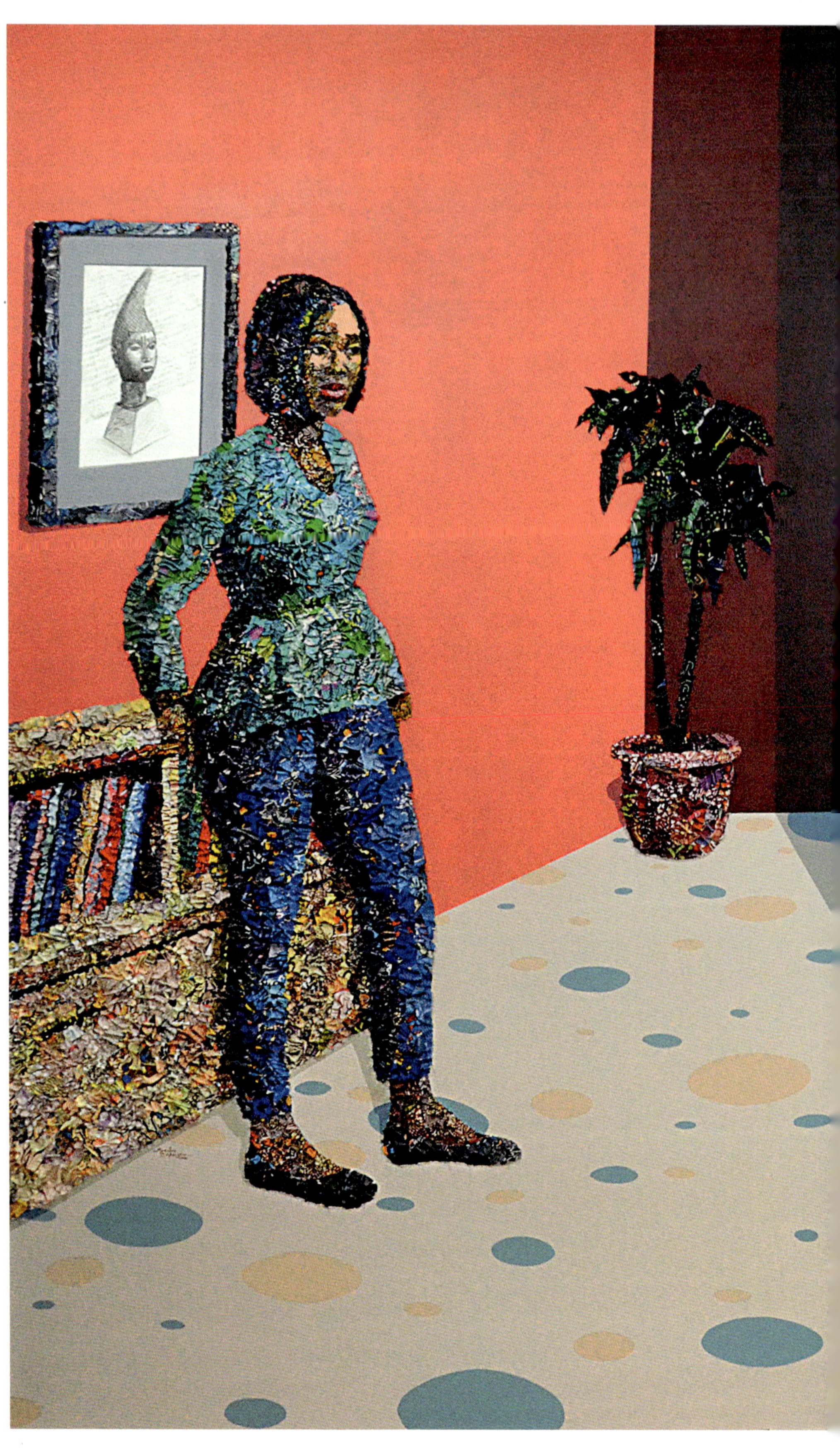

Rhythm of Evolving Story (diptych), 2020,
mixed media,
96 × 156 in.

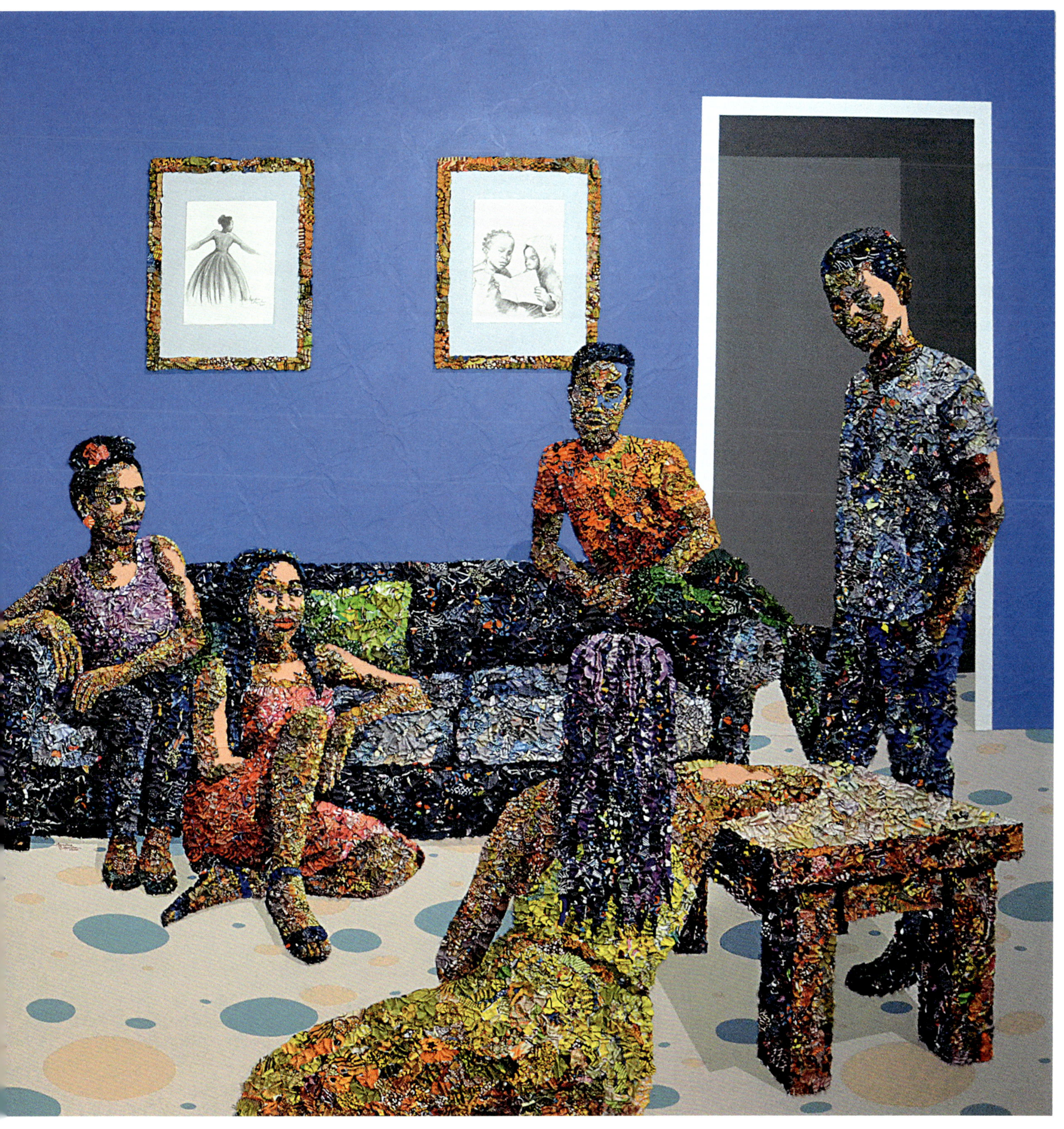

DAUGHTERS OF ESAN

The series 'Daughters of Esan' is a generational story of timeless ambition of one woman who saw into the future. This body of work depicts five generations of women (Akpojotor's great-grandmother, her grandmother, her mother, herself and her child) with roots from Esan – an ethnic group that occupies central Edo State.

Akpojotor chronicles her family's journey to the fulfilment of the radical vision of her great-grandmother – Eboheide Anare Ikhisemojie. Ikhisemojie, who was born in 1910, wanted to receive an education but was unable to do so. Her strong desire to be educated set the tone and paved the way for the following generations to reach various academic levels.

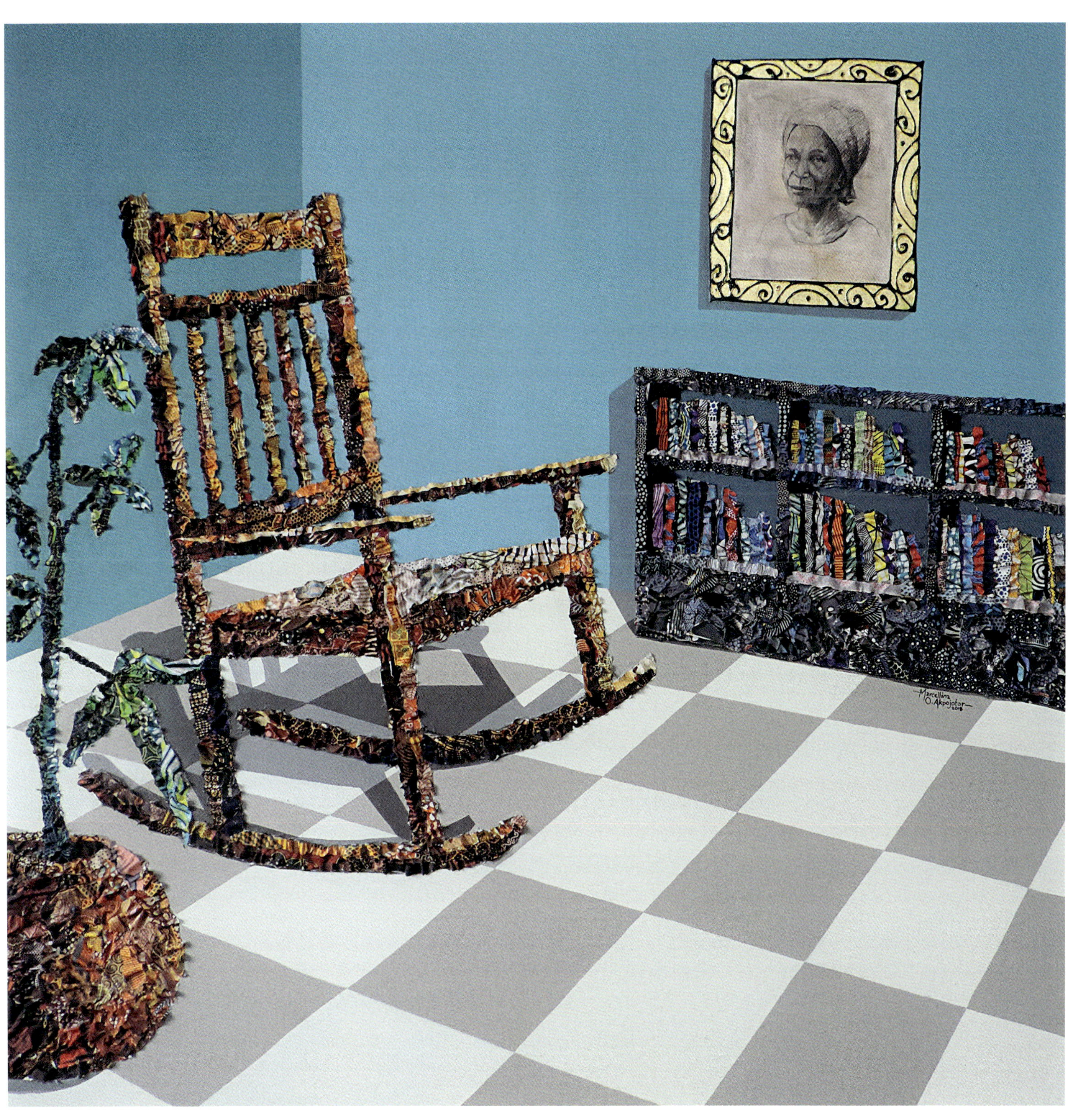

Daughter of Esan (First Generation), 2018,
fabric and acrylic on canvas,
48 × 48 in.

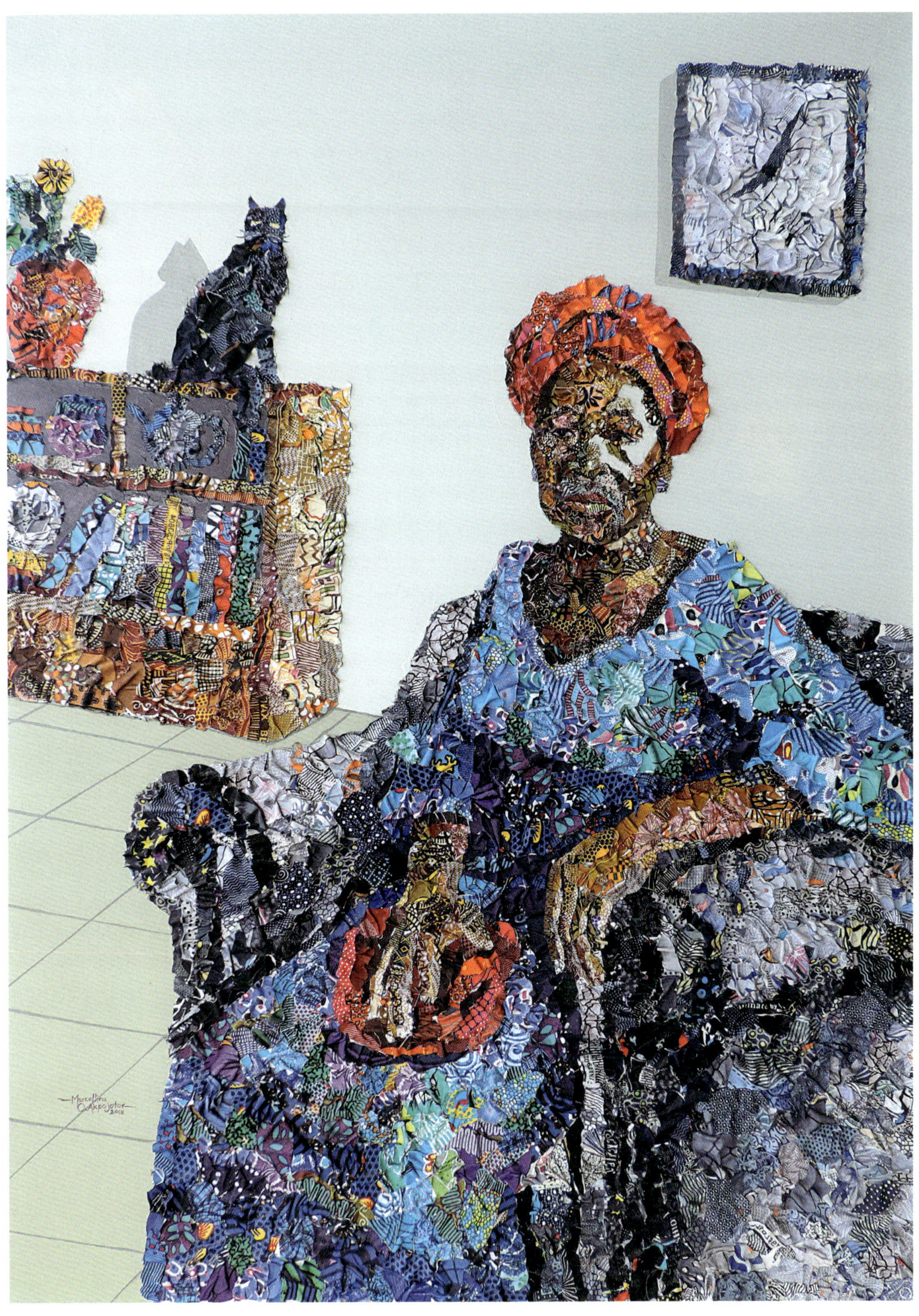

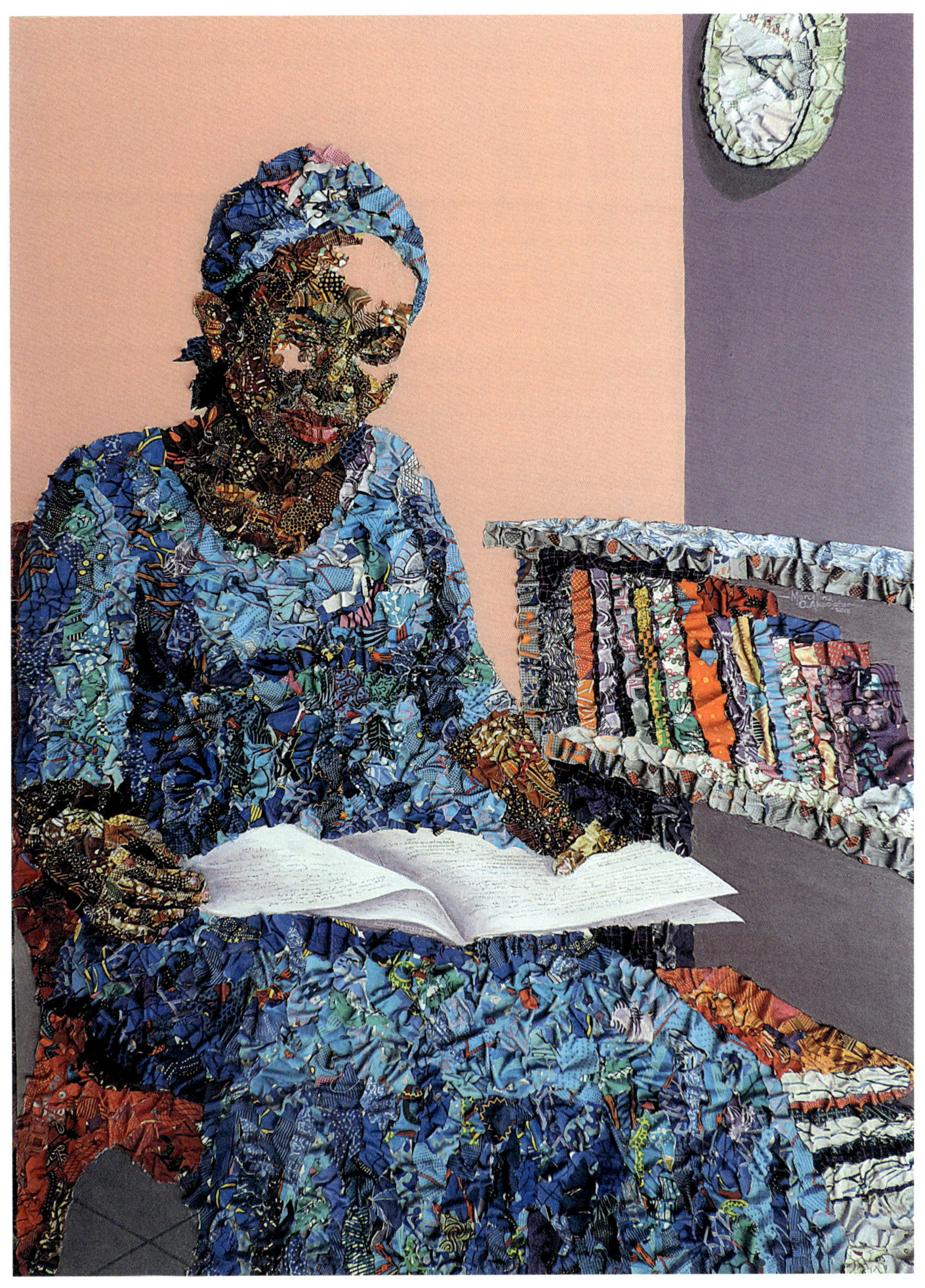

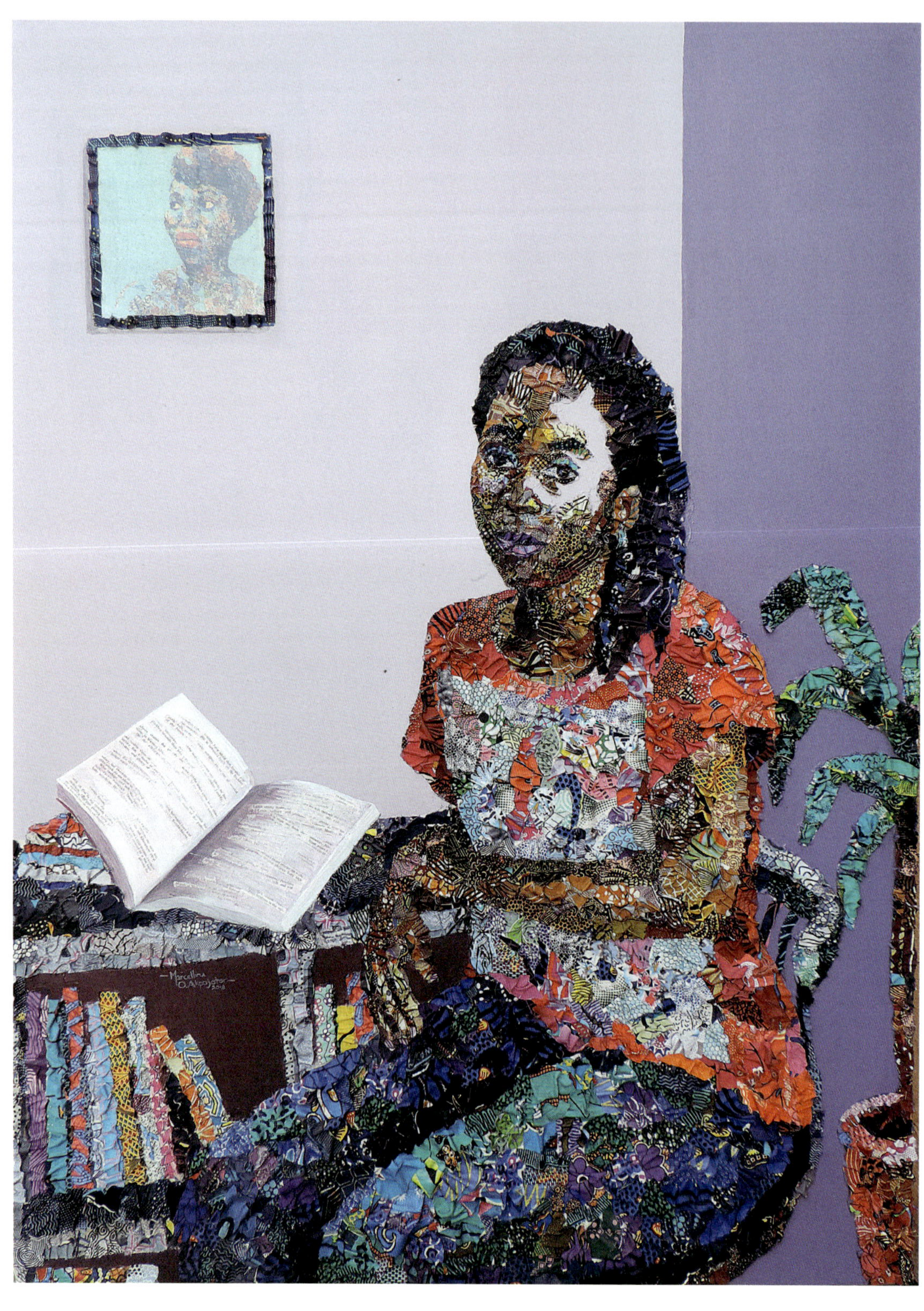

Daughter of Esan (Fourth Generation), 2018,
fabric and acrylic on canvas,
48 × 36 in.

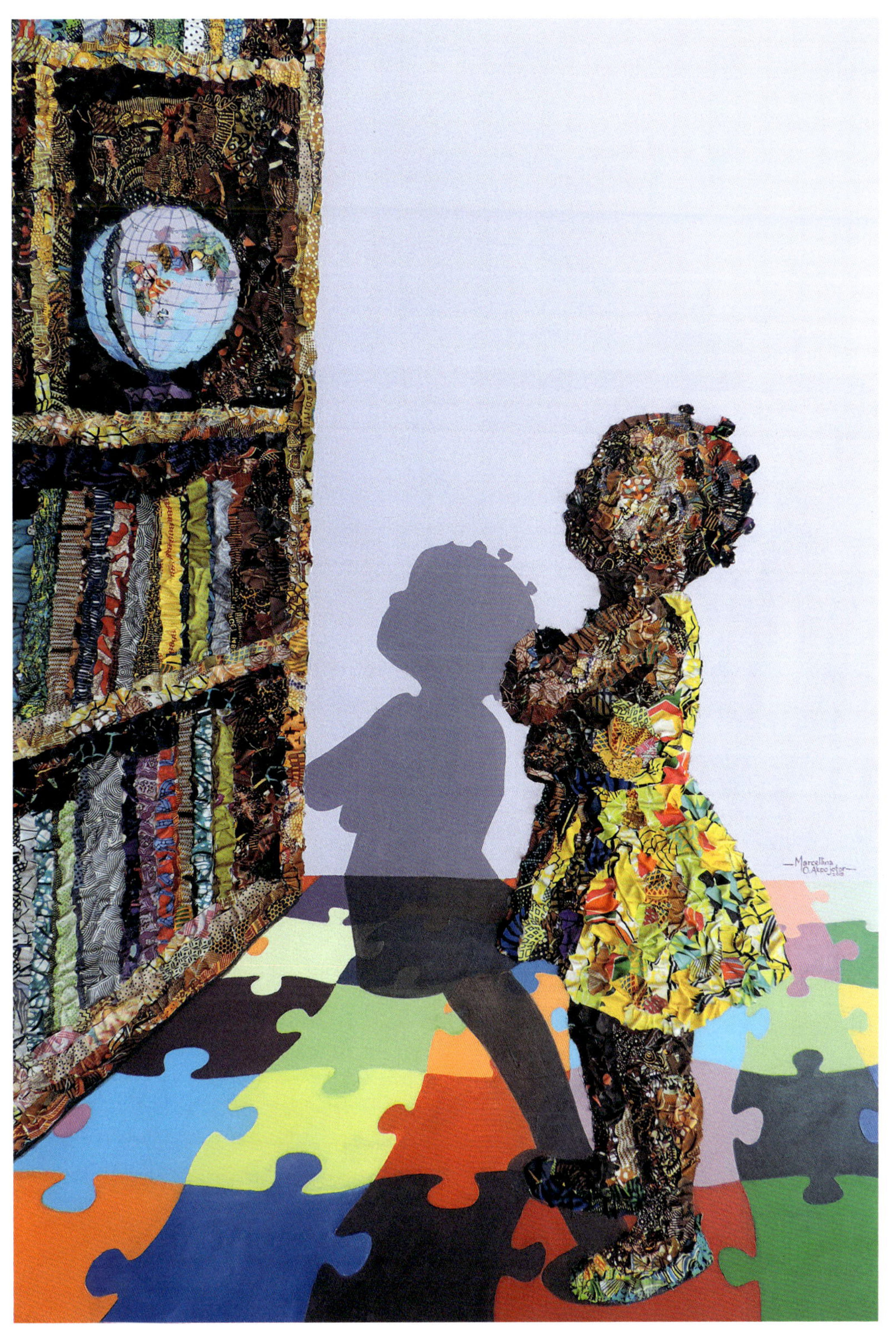

Daughter of Esan (Fifth Generation),
2018, fabric and acrylic on canvas,
48 × 36 in.

JOY OF MORE WORLDS

Employing collaging and traditional painting techniques, Marcellina Akpojotor's work dialogues with familial history, the evolving nature of archives and an intimate celebration of memories and generational legacy.

Building upon her current explorations of her maternal bloodline across generations as well as her series 'Kesiena's Diary', this body of work focuses on the artist's daughter, presenting us with scenes of intimacy and family life. Through familiar and idyllic scenes, Akpojotor takes the viewer on a journey through parenthood – a journey that leaps across time, documenting intimate lives in stages. Here, she creates vivid compositions focused on capturing the immediacy of a moment, engaged simultaneously in the act of creating and archiving memories.

In 'Joy of More Worlds', Akpojotor draws from the domestic, creating snapshots of daily life: from acts of play to scenes of support and intimacy. These moments, seemingly frozen in time, allow the viewer a glance into private spaces, weaving narratives of childhood and growth.

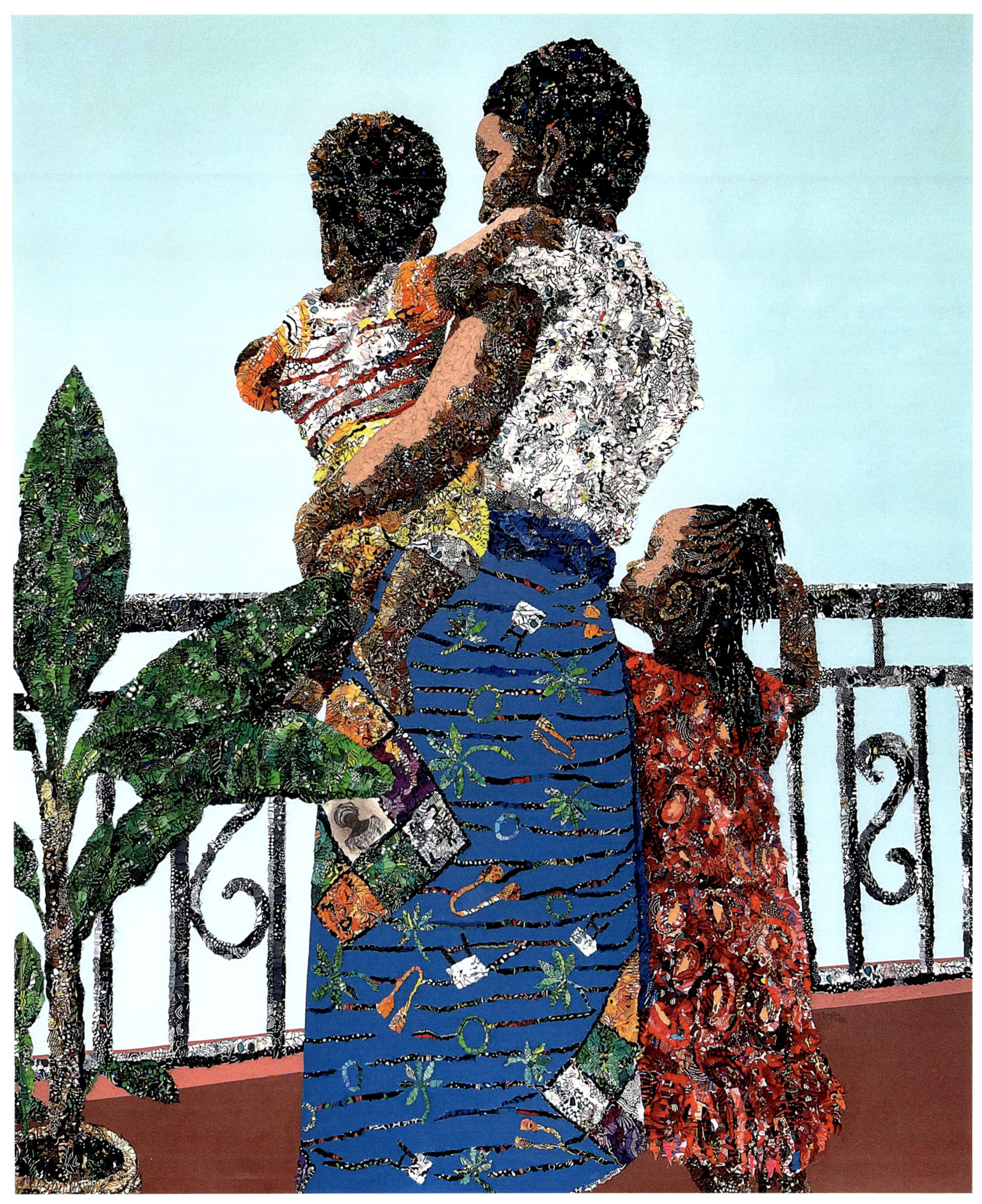

Weekend with Grandma, 2022,
fabric, charcoal on paper and
acrylic on canvas,
96 × 76 in.

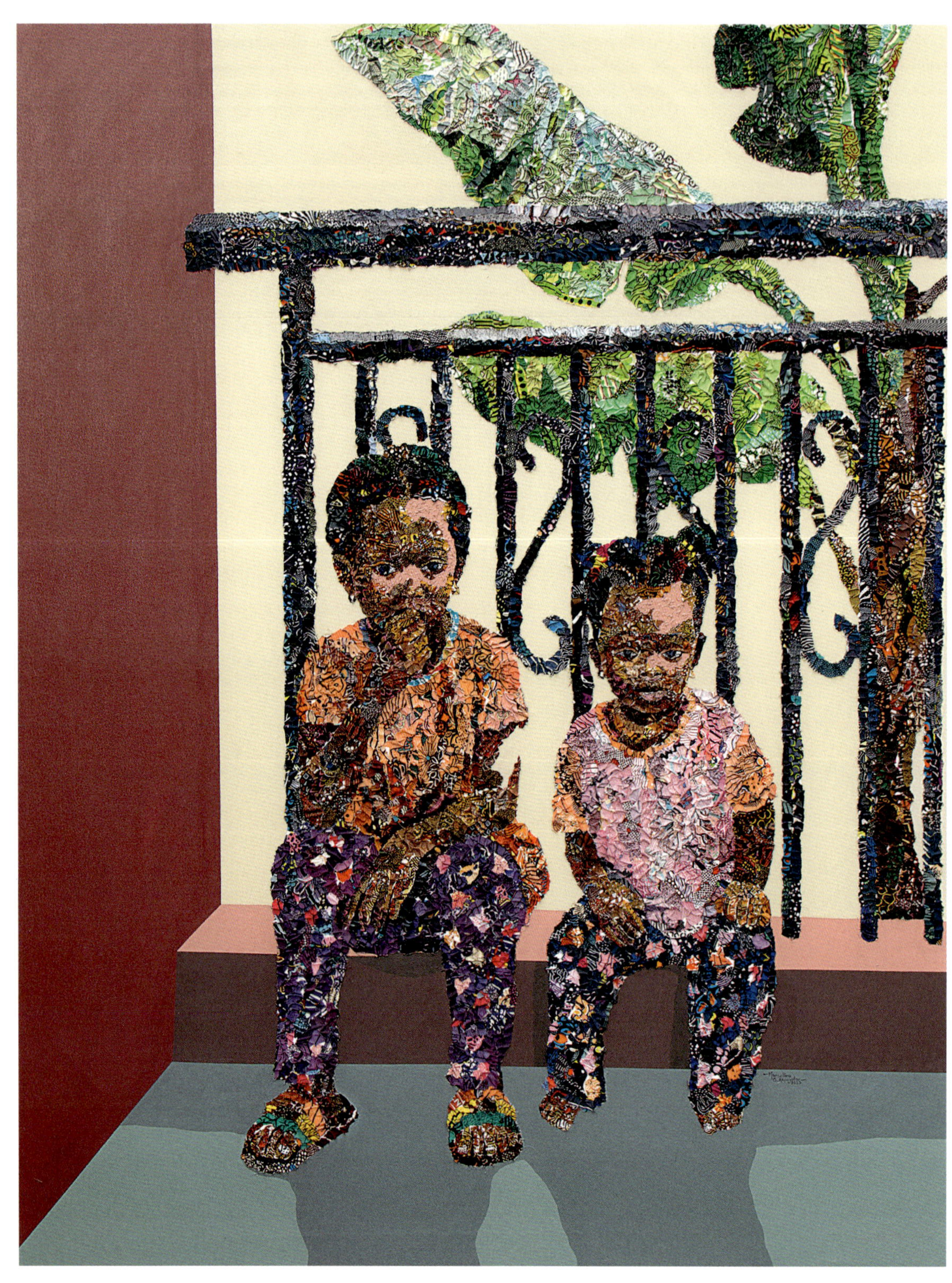

Pyjama Sisters, 2023,
fabric and acrylic on canvas,
77 × 60 in.

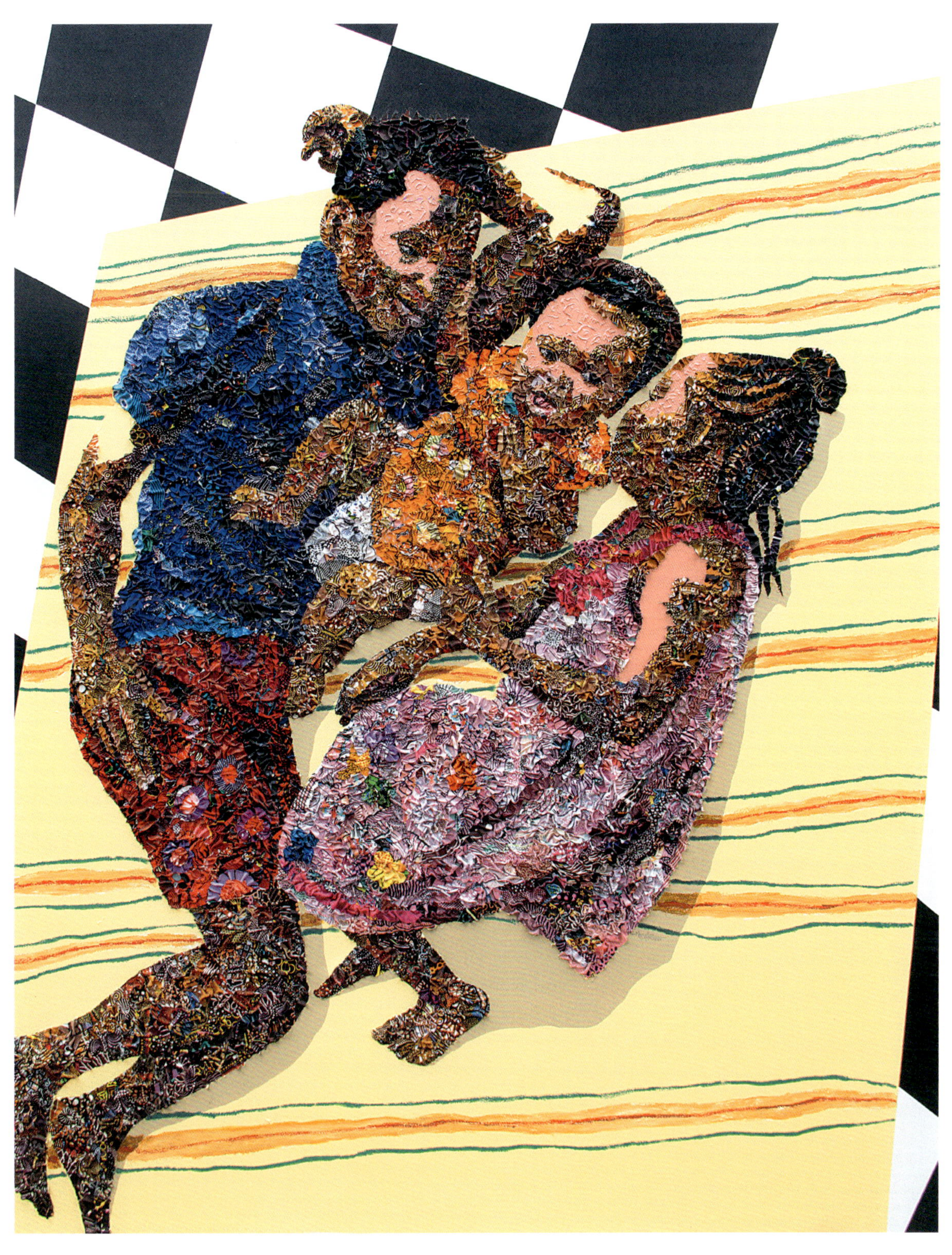

Bloom and Joy, 2023,
fabric, acrylic and oil stick on canvas,
77 × 60 in.

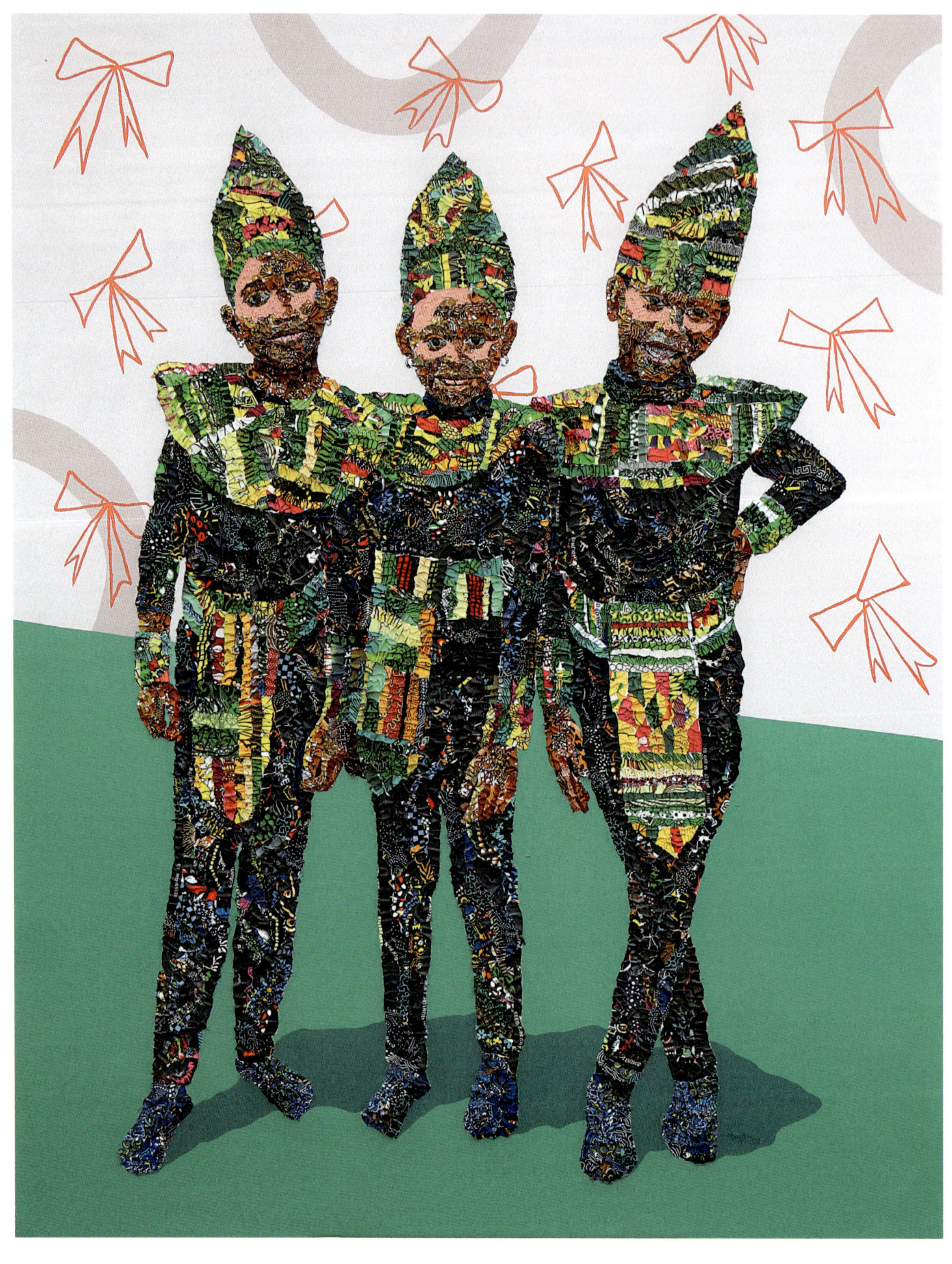

Love for Country (WOW Day), 2023,
fabric and acrylic on canvas,
77 × 60 in.

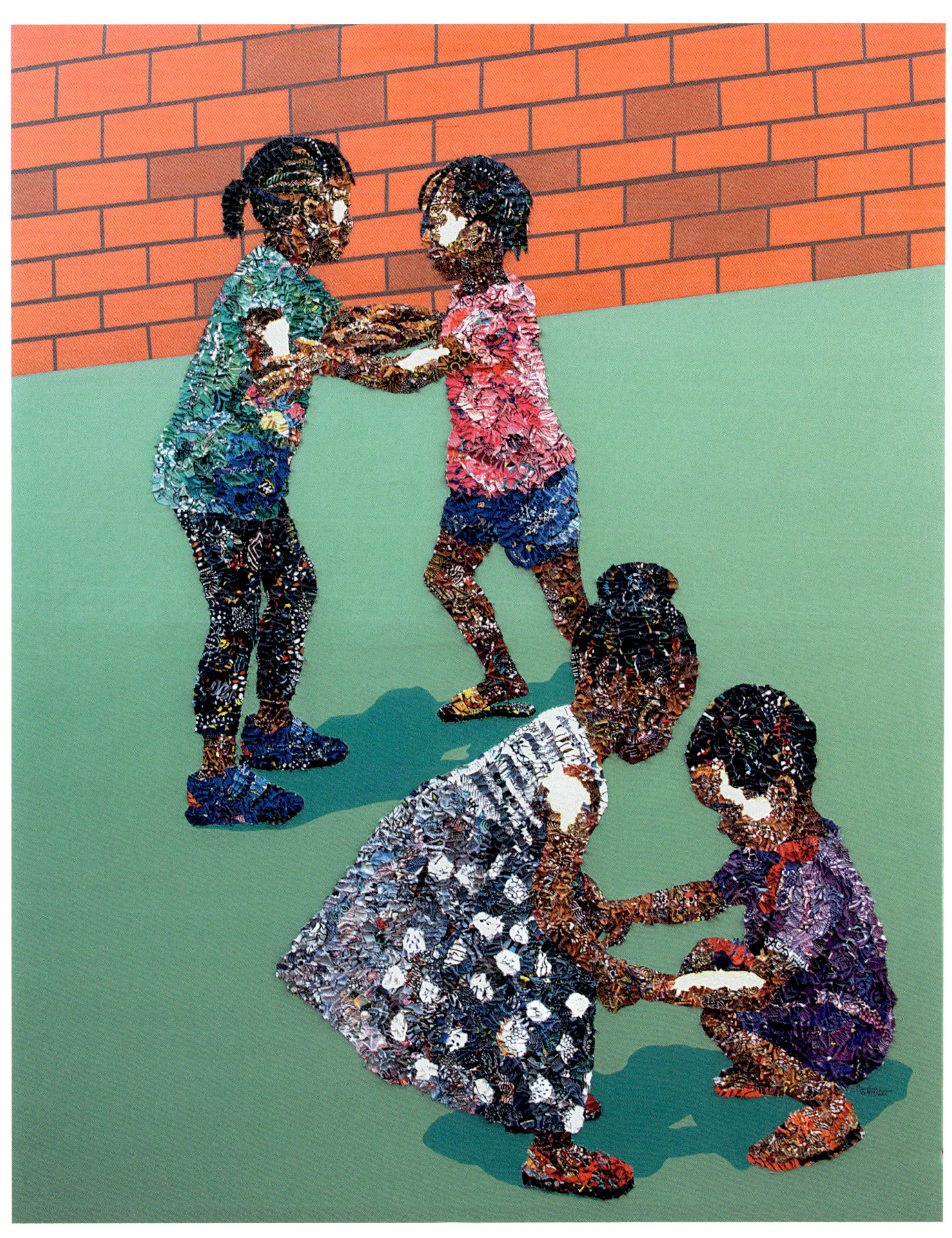

Saturday Visit, 2023,
fabric and acrylic on canvas,
77 × 60 in.

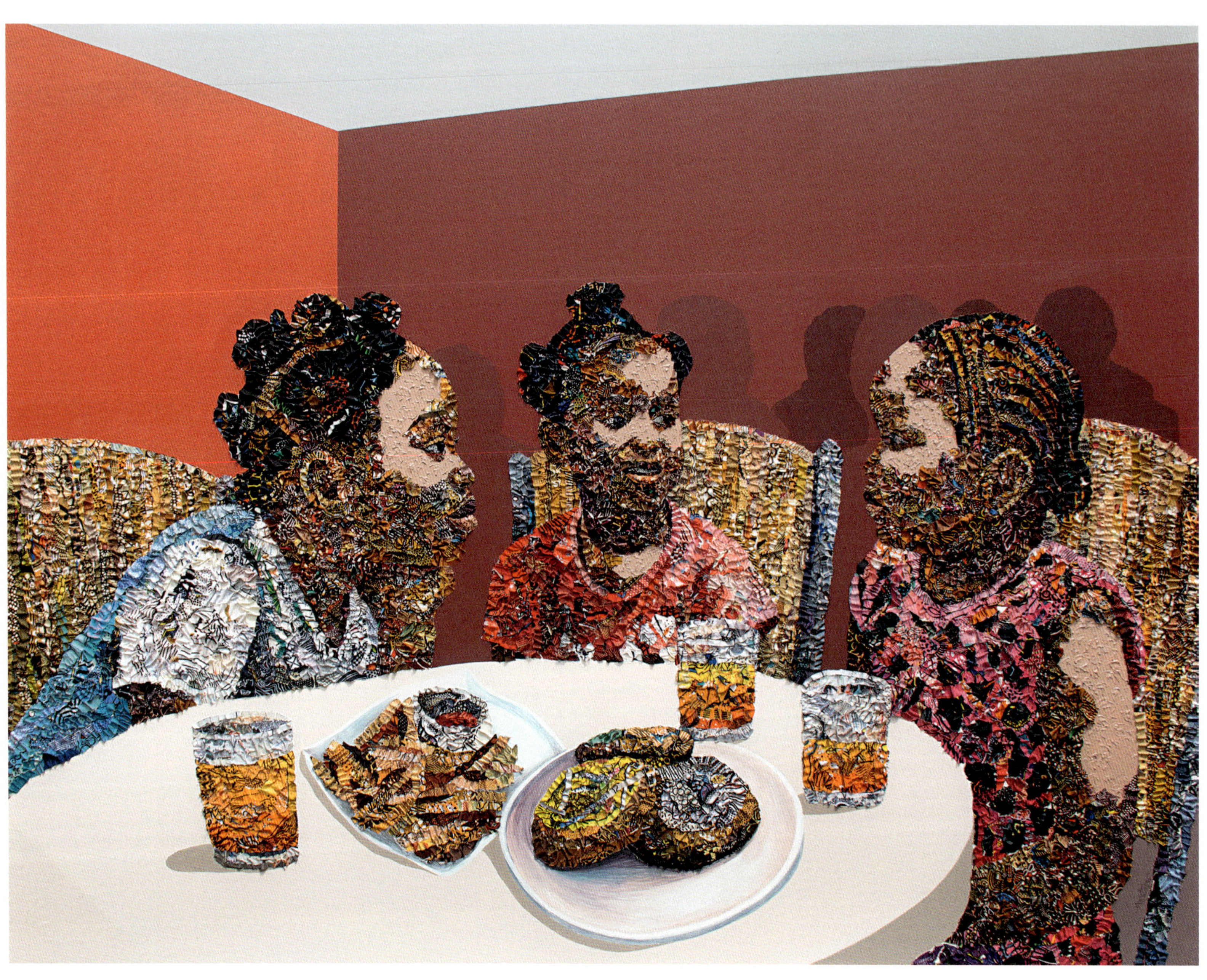

Good Times, 2023,
fabric and acrylic on canvas,
60 × 77 in.

Sweet Holiday, 2023,
fabric and acrylic on canvas,
60 × 77 in.

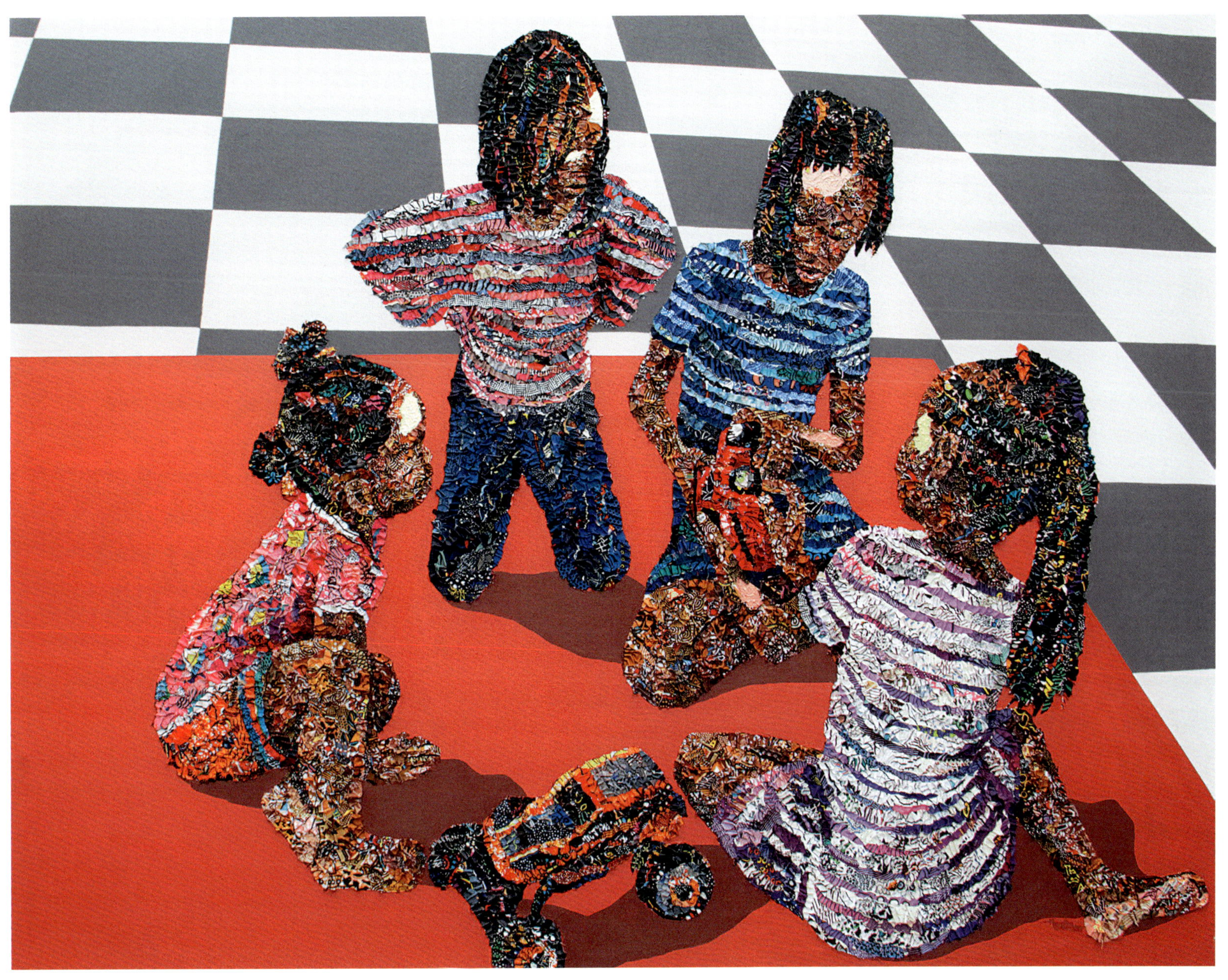

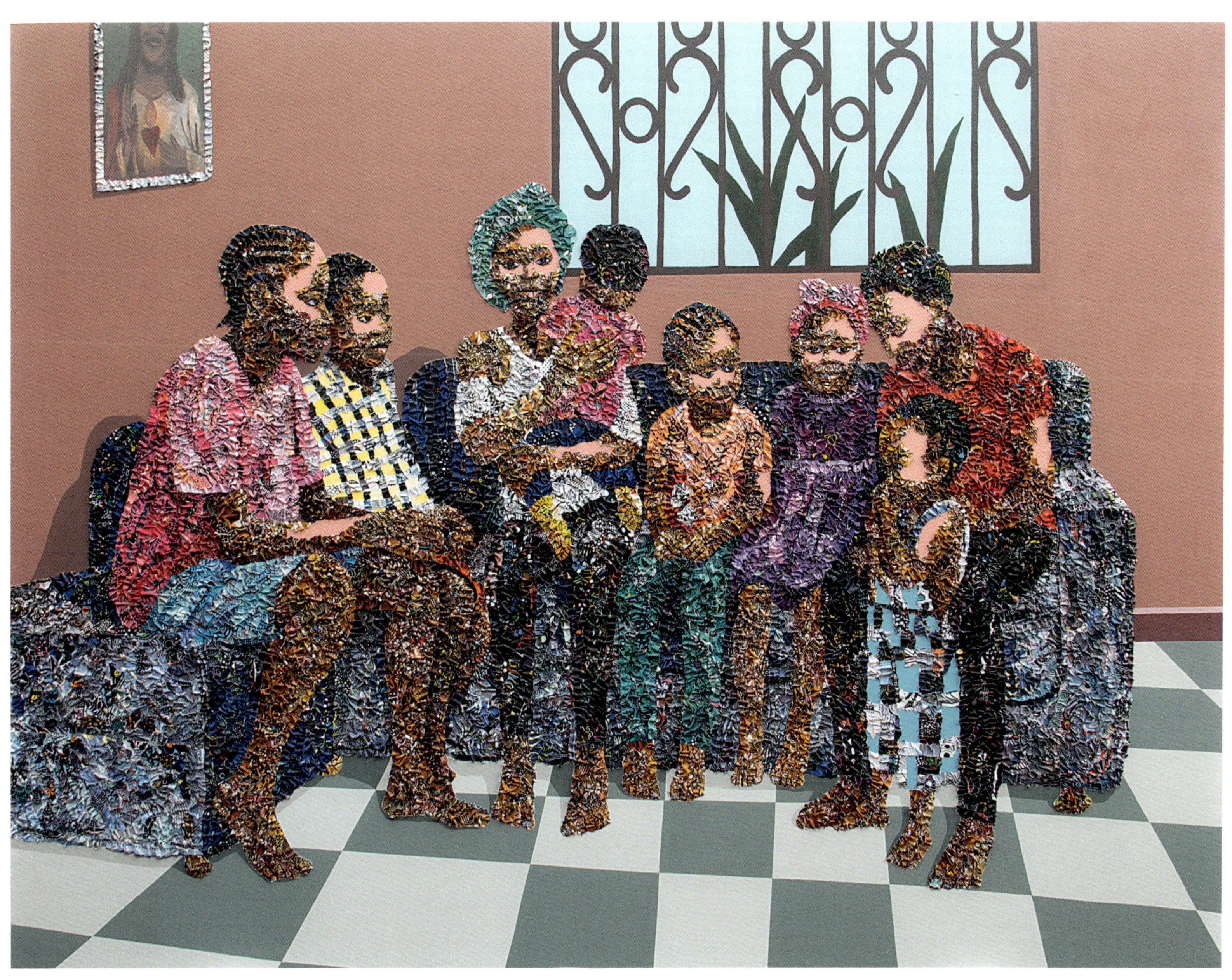

KESIENA'S DIARY

The works in 'Kesiena's Diary' are rooted in ideas of affection and the familial, engaging notions of lineage and legacy. Building upon Marcellina Akpojotor's previous explorations of her maternal bloodline across generations, this body of work also focuses on her daughter.

The series dialogues with genealogy, being part of a larger exploration of Akpojotor's matriarchal lineage. Situated against her great-grandmother's radical vision for literacy and the subsequent realisation of this vision in varying degrees among later generations, the paintings feature scenes of study and tutoring, echoing the artist's own fascination with education as a tool for liberation and empowerment.

Done in her signature mix of fabric collage and painting, 'Kesiena's Diary' features densely layered and intricately detailed characters shown in composition against flat, brightly coloured backgrounds. The idea of the familial space here is one rooted deeply in acts of companionship – a scene of mother and daughter bent studiously over schoolwork, or of a father riding a bicycle with his daughter. These moments become a way for the artist to relish the proximity that childhood offers as well as a means to record the passing of time.

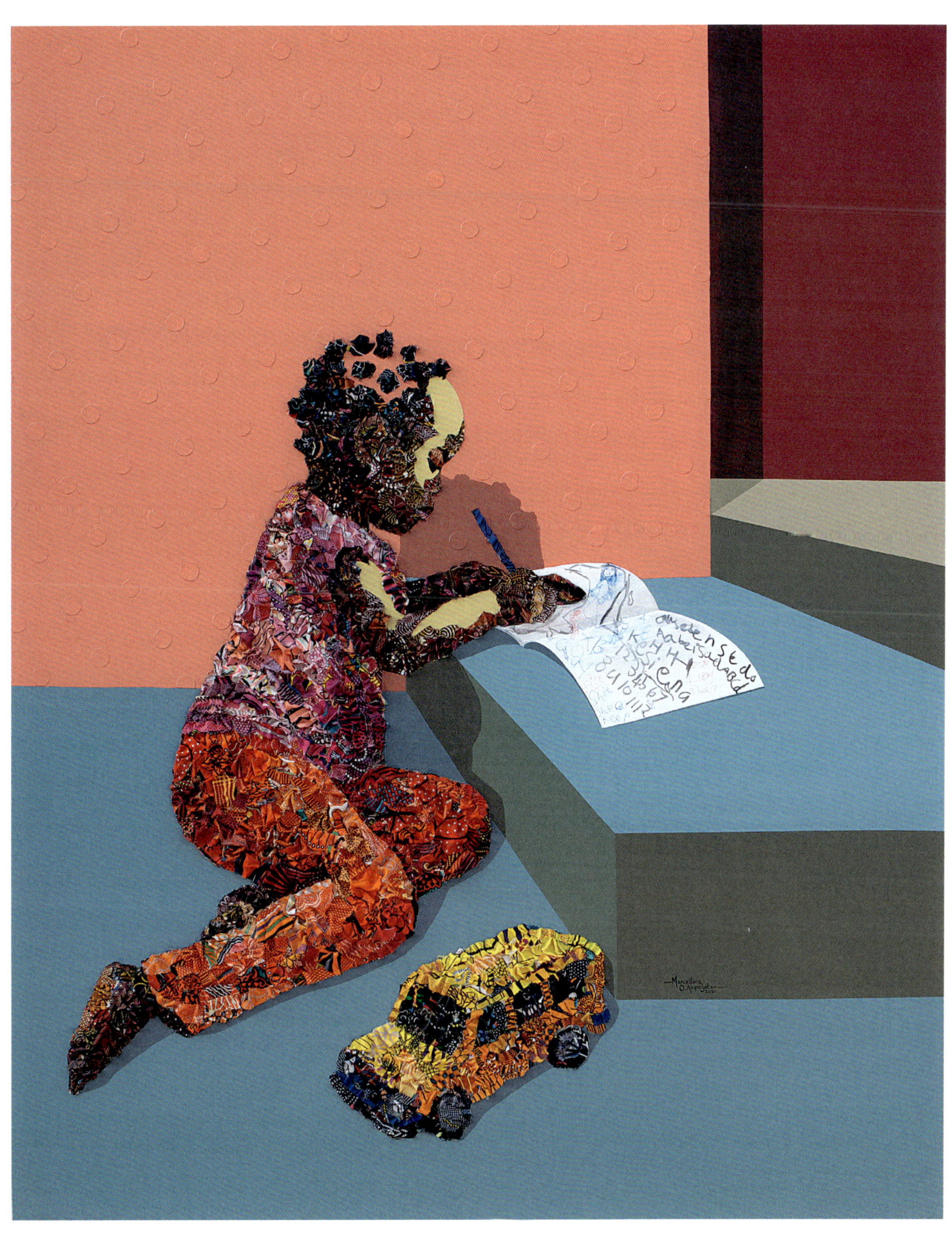

Letters and Doodles, 2021,
fabric, paper and acrylic on canvas,
60 × 48 in.

Papa's Girl, 2021,
fabric, paper and acrylic on canvas,
60 × 48 in.

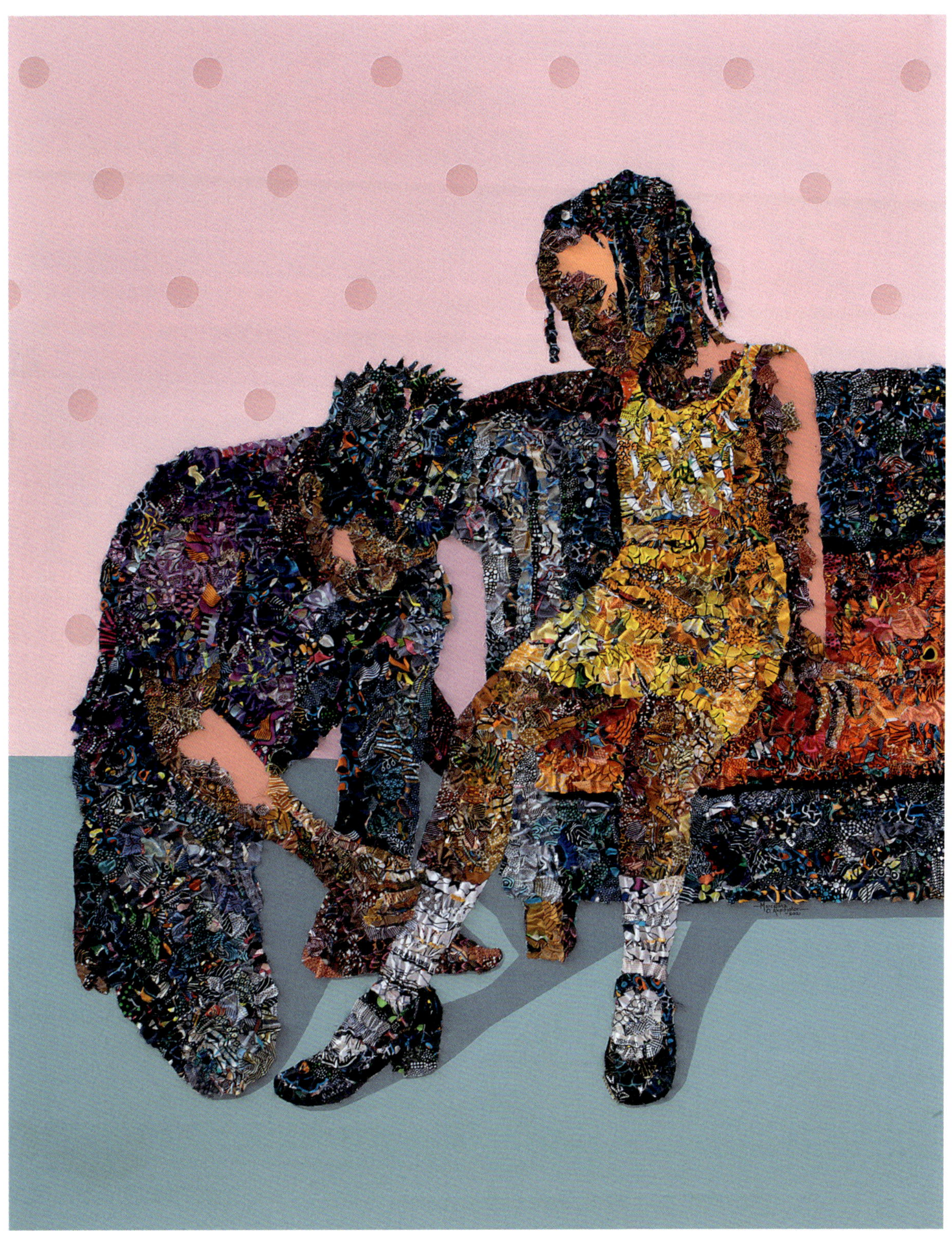

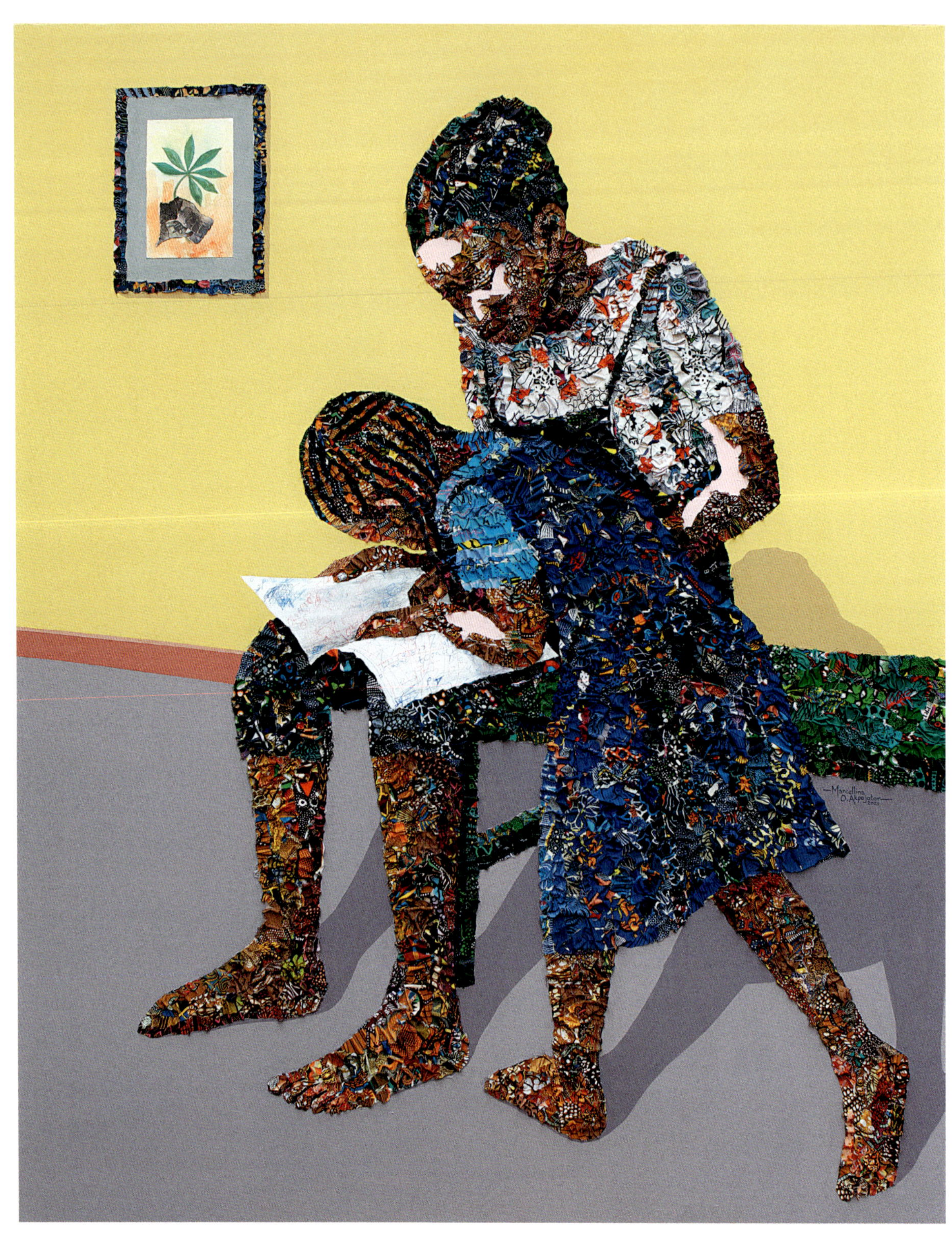

After School Hour, 2021,
fabric and acrylic on canvas,
60 × 48 in.

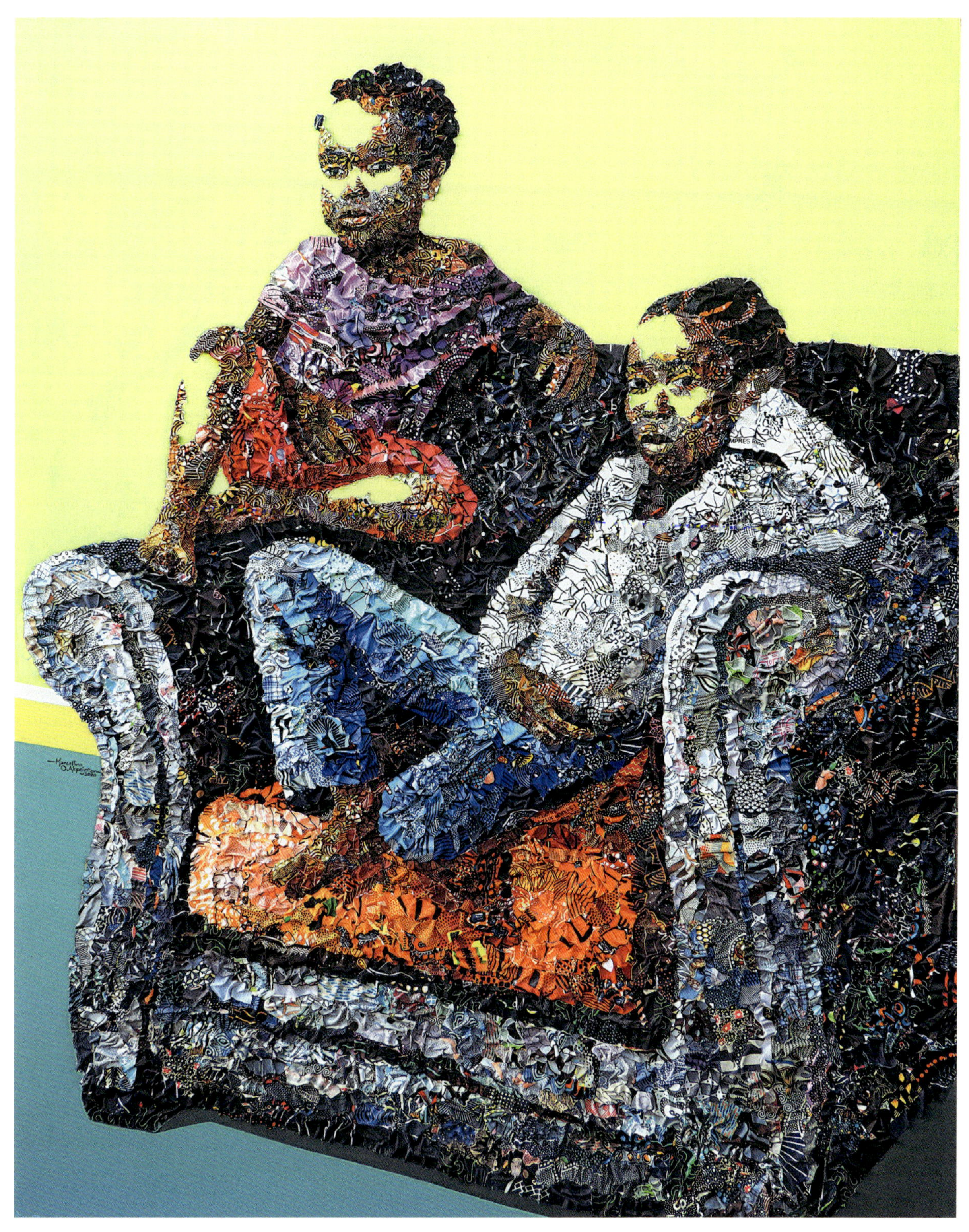

Ovoke, 2019–2020,
fabric and acrylic on canvas,
60 × 48 in.

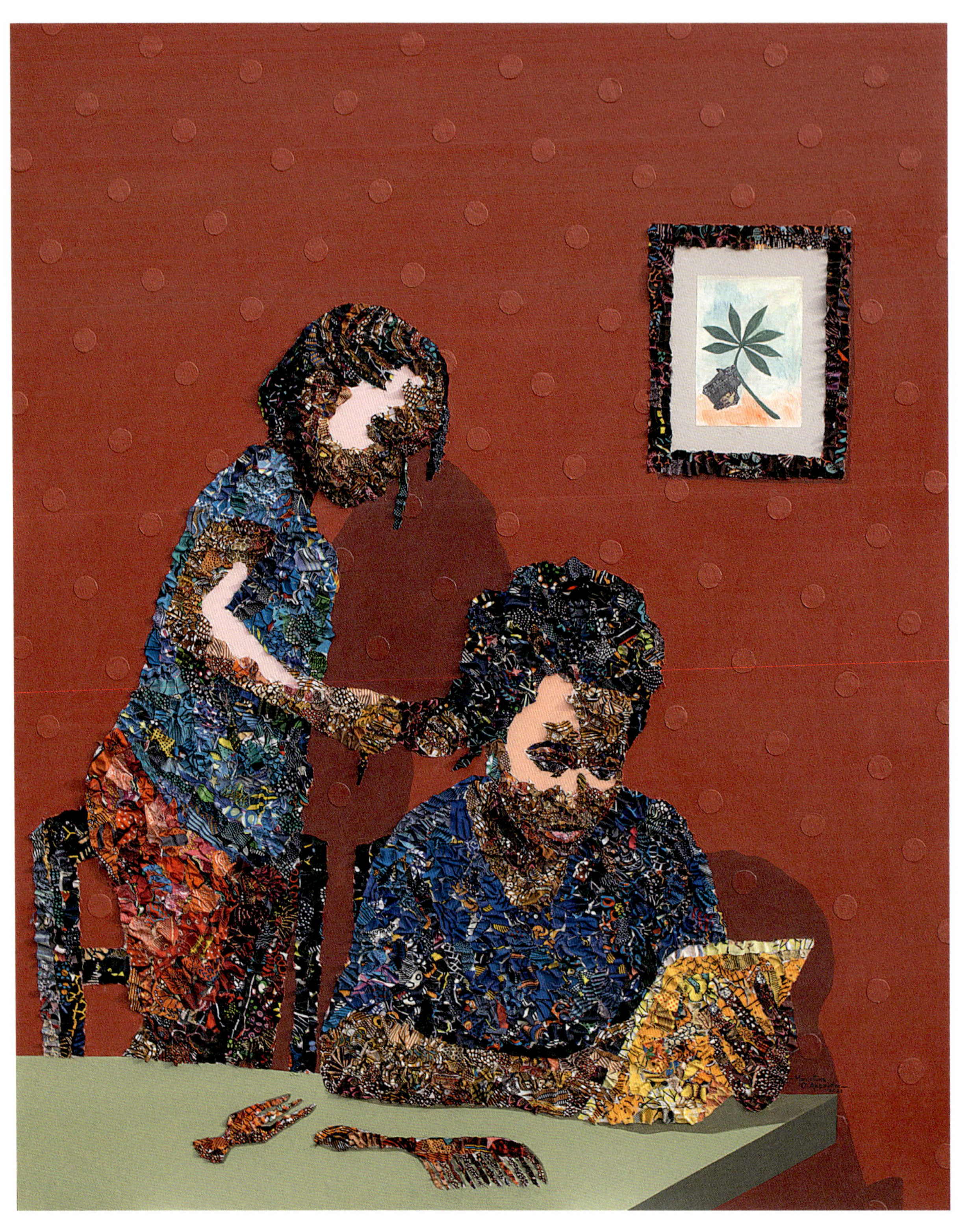

Beauty in the Curls, 2021,
fabric, paper and acrylic on canvas,
60 × 48 in.

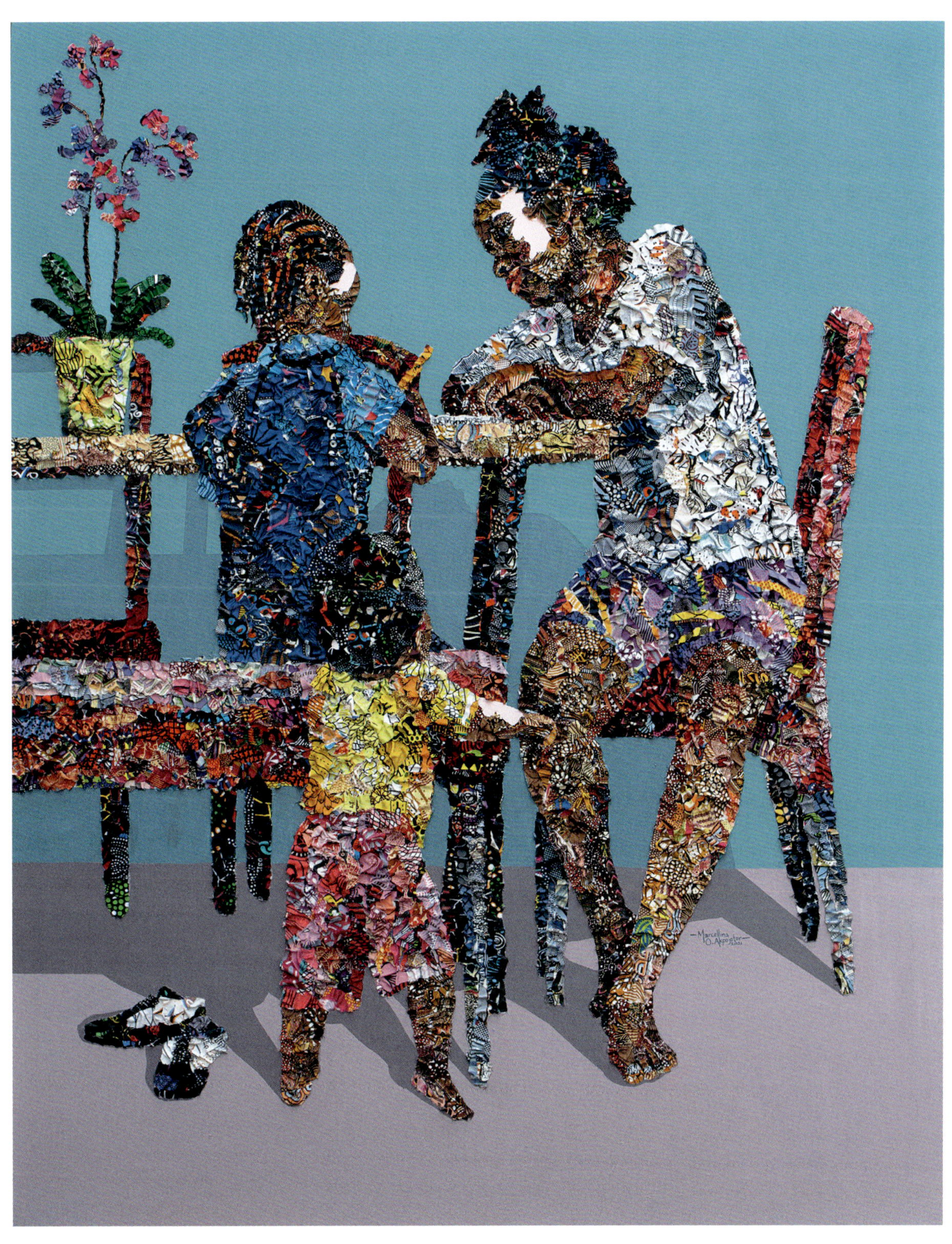

The Dining Table, 2021,
fabric, paper and acrylic on canvas,
60 × 48 in.

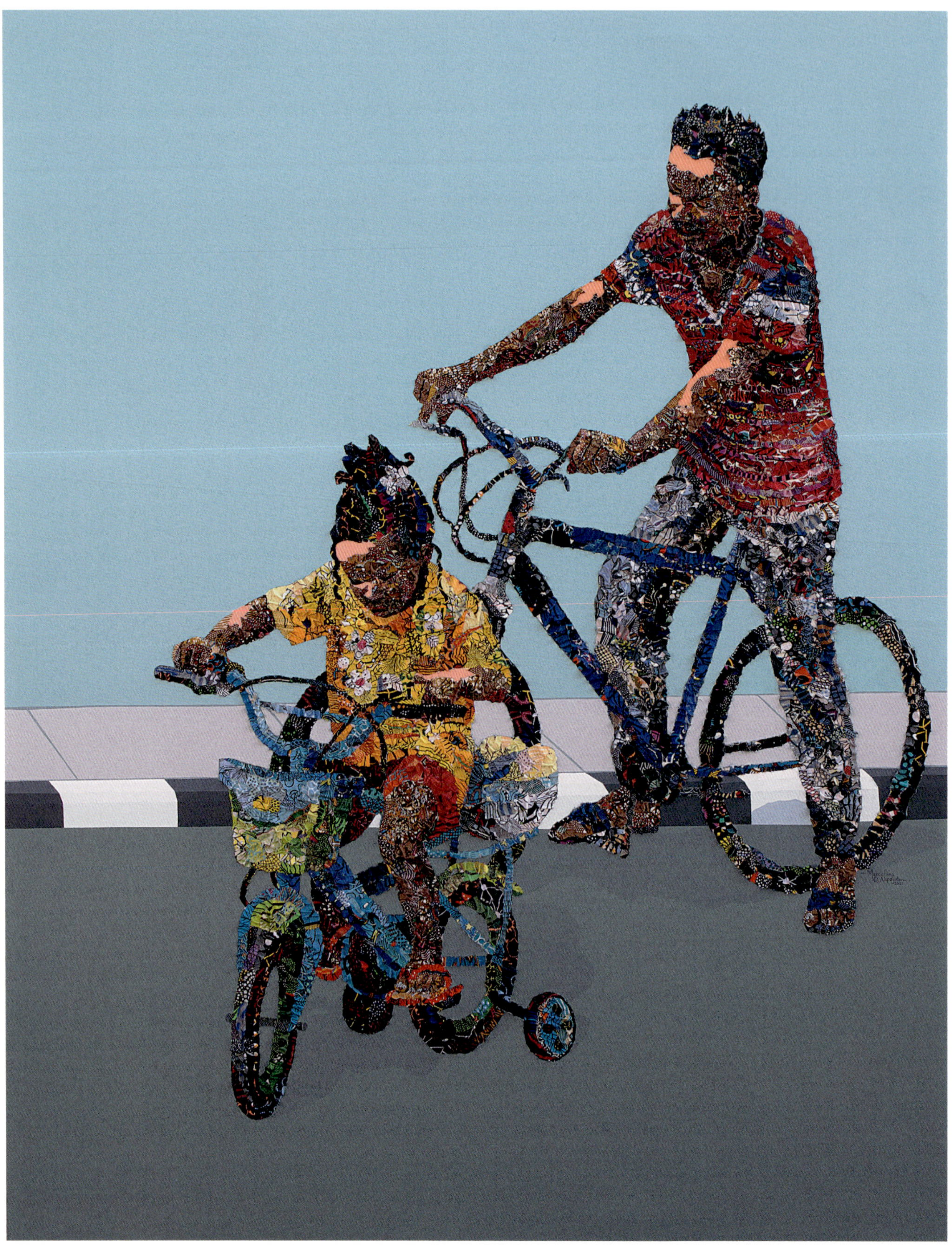

Wheels on the Street, 2021,
fabric and acrylic on canvas,
77 × 60 in.

Fly Baby, Fly!, 2021,
fabric and acrylic on canvas,
77 × 60 in.

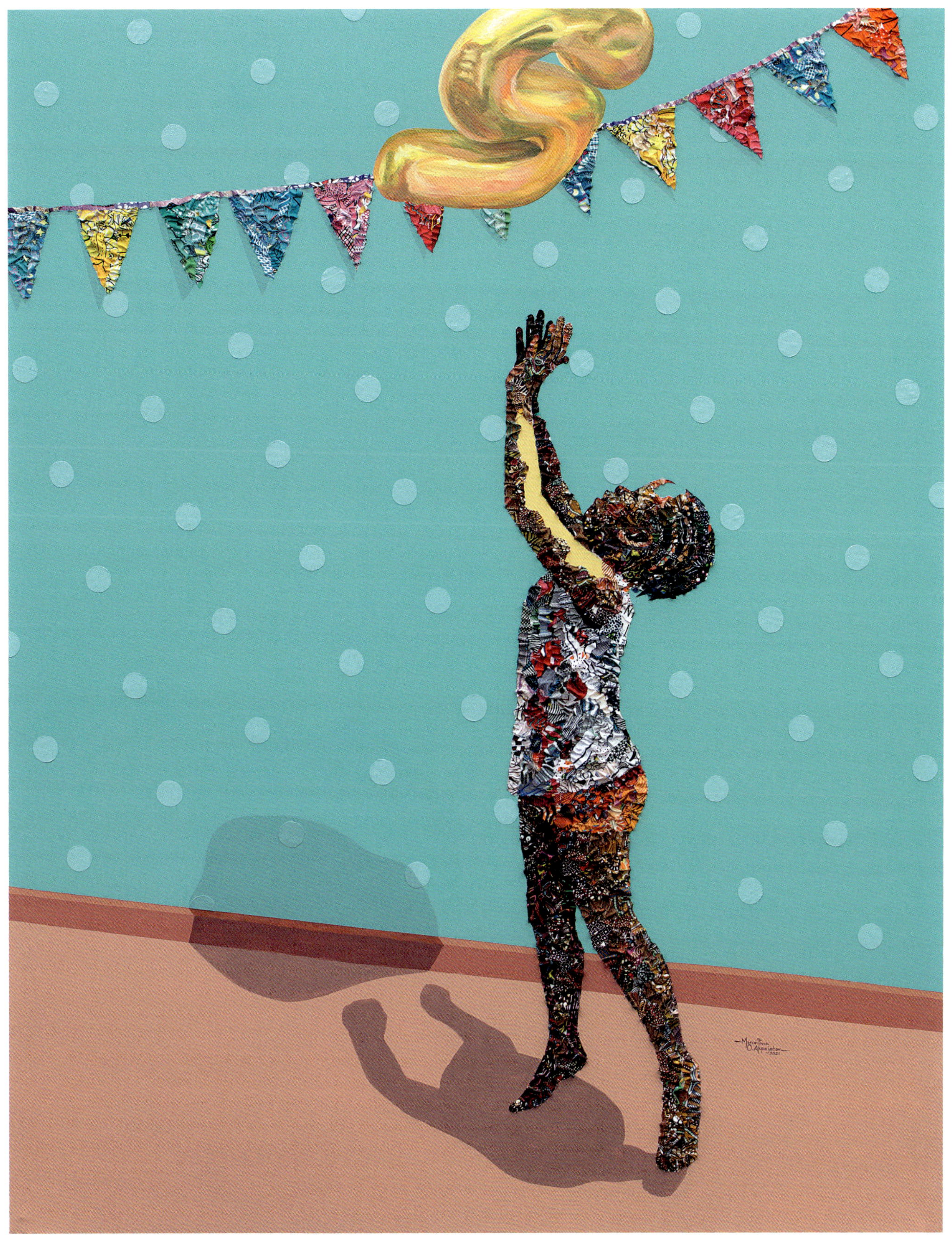

ODE TO BEAUTIFUL MEMORIES

'Ode to Beautiful Memories' is an ongoing dialogue on familial history, the evolving nature of archives and an intimate celebration of memories and generational legacy. The series functions as both a re-engagement with a personal history as well as an act of remembrance and commemoration, serving as a monument and testament to past lives and unfolding futures. Drawing heavily on oral traditions as well as archival material, Marcellina Akpojotor creates densely layered work that delicately explores the life and realities of her late great-grandmother Eboheide 'Dede' Anare Ikhisemojie, estimated to have been born in 1910 and who died in 1992.

In understanding the life of the woman whose strong desire to be educated set the tone and paved the way for the following generations to reach various academic levels, the artist aims to explore and reimagine events – from the quotidian to the iconic – which marked the realities of her existence. Events such as the colonisation and amalgamation of Nigeria, its subsequent independence, the Nigerian Civil War and the women's rights movement of that period, as well as her personal politics and daily life, form vital contexts in Akpojotor's reading of family history.

Working in her signature style of using ankara fabric to create highly textured paintings, the artist explores and echoes the commemorative nature of traditional fabrics and their attendant possibilities as repositories of history and intimate stories. Here, the fabrics take on archival and contemporary qualities, drawing from their storied past and contemporary relevance. Archival photographs and symbolic motifs also play an important role in mapping out layered landscapes of history. Drawing on old family photographs sourced from family albums and the internet, 'Ode to Beautiful Memories' presents the archive as living and embodied, capable of storing and activating personal histories and legacies while also referencing the ageing process and their ultimate temporality.

In 'Ode to Beautiful Memories', the artist honours the life and legacy of her great-grandmother and imagines the series as a monument – an act of re-memory and commemoration. With this body of work, Akpojotor aims to not only engage with and examine the storied reality and lived experiences of her great-grandmother's life, but also to document and immortalise her memory for existing and coming generations in her family, through an unfolding, contemporary archive. In her exploration of past events, the artist also invites viewers to critically engage with their individual and collective histories in a bid to understand the way they shape current and future realities.

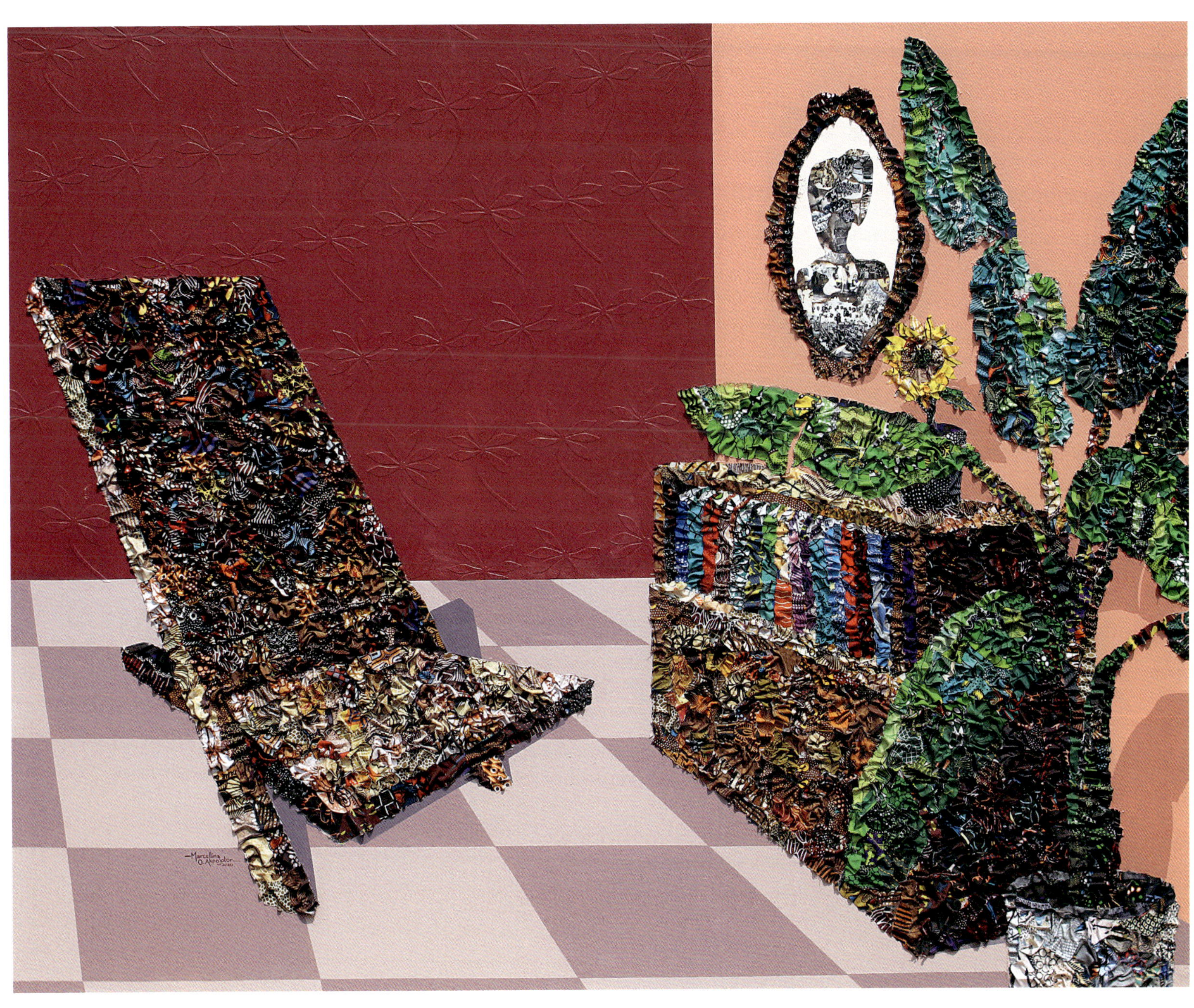

Dede's Corner, 2020,
fabric, paper and acrylic on canvas,
48 × 60 in.

Blooming Red Soil, 2020,
fabric, paper and acrylic on canvas,
48 × 60 in.

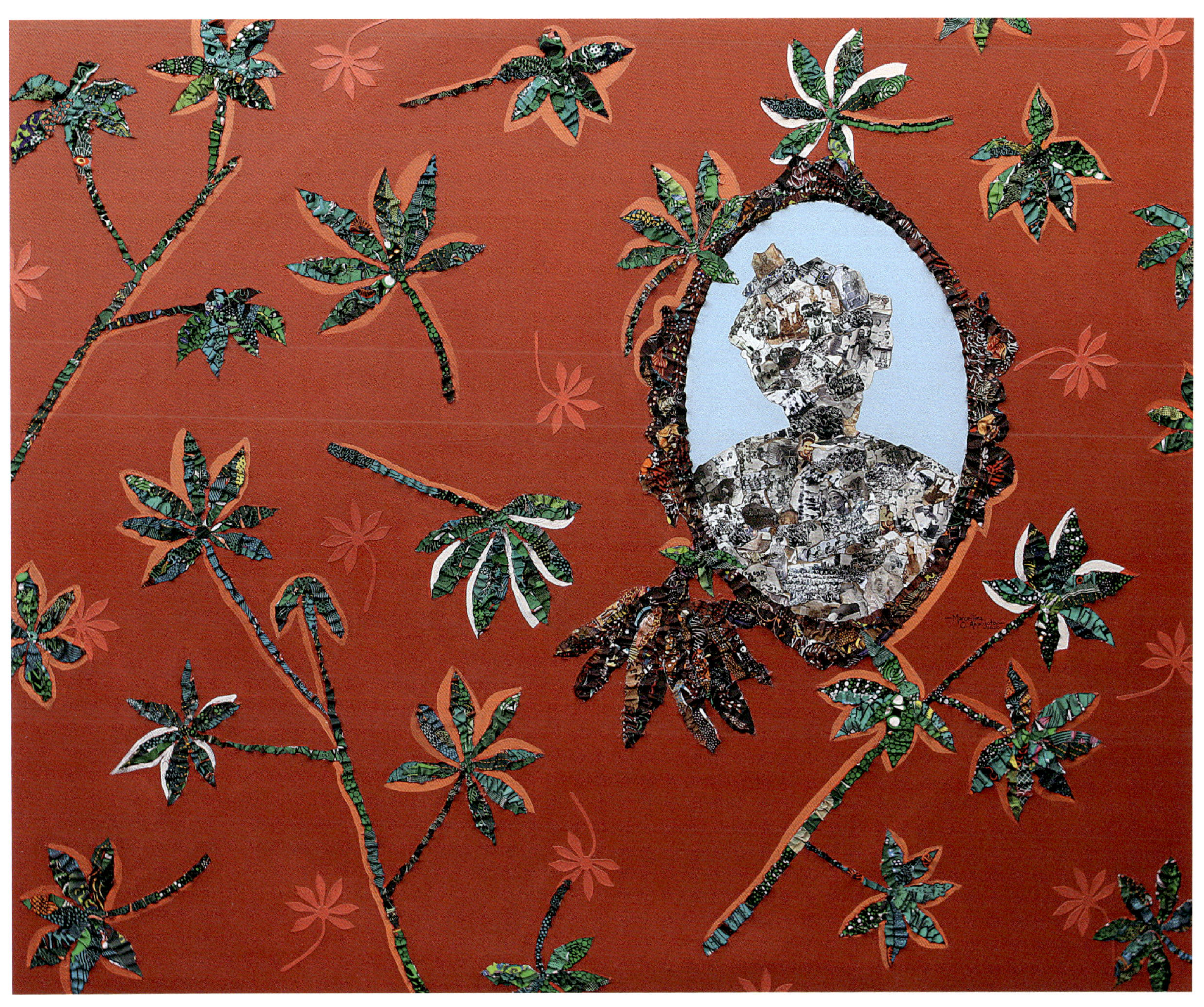

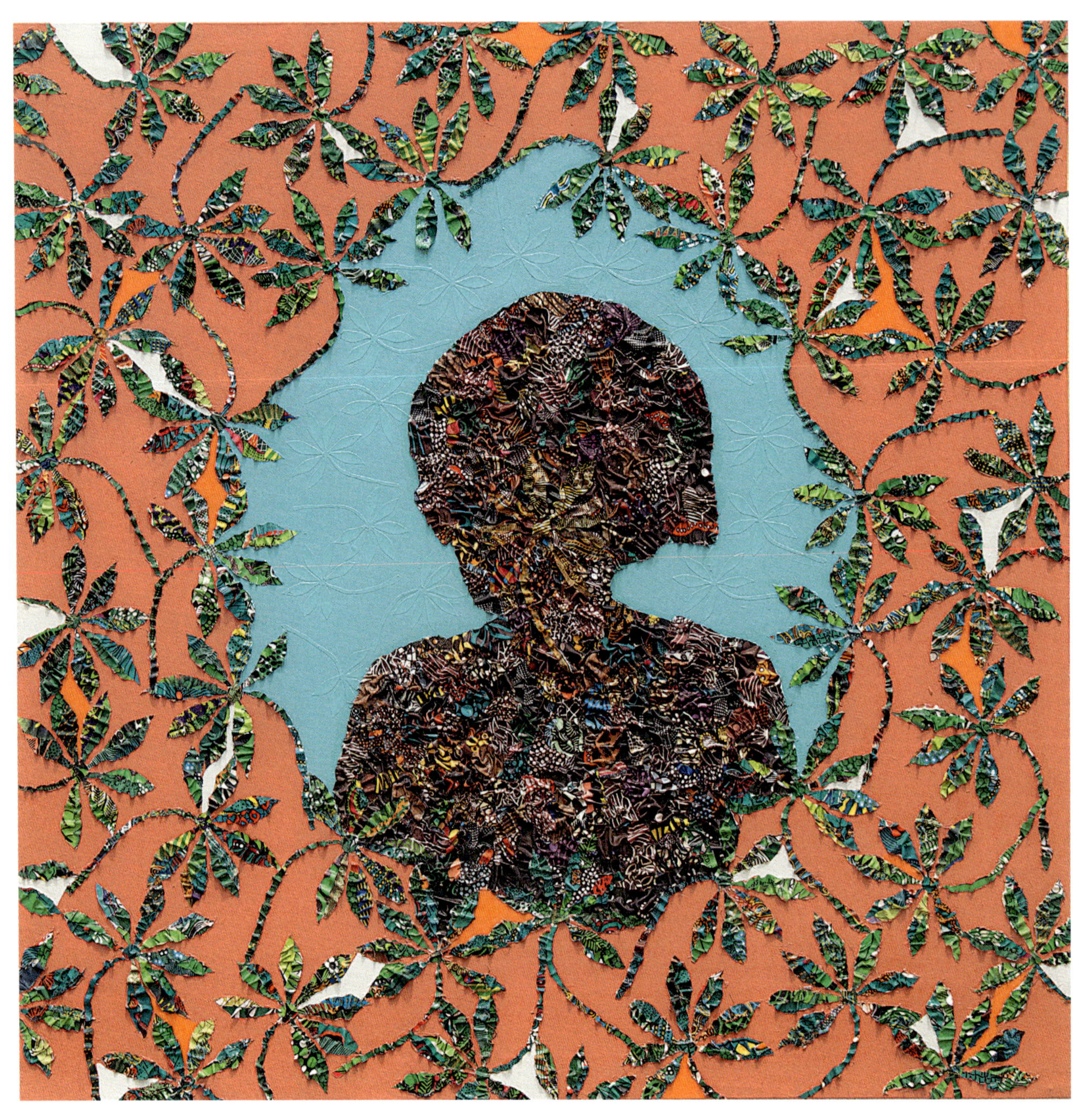

Dede II, 2021,
fabric, paper and acrylic on canvas,
48 × 48 in.

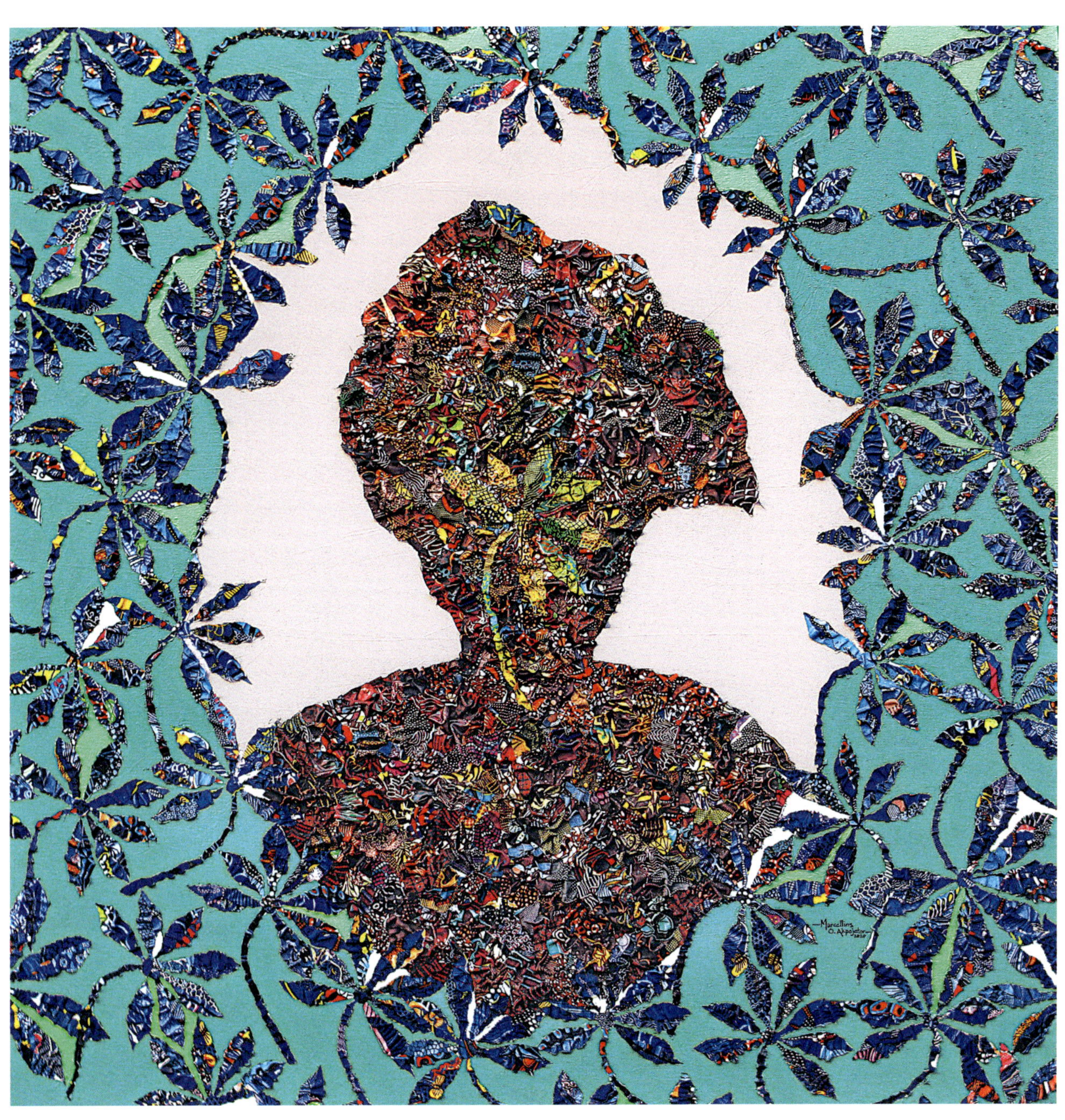

Dede I, 2020,
fabric and acrylic on canvas,
48 × 48 in.

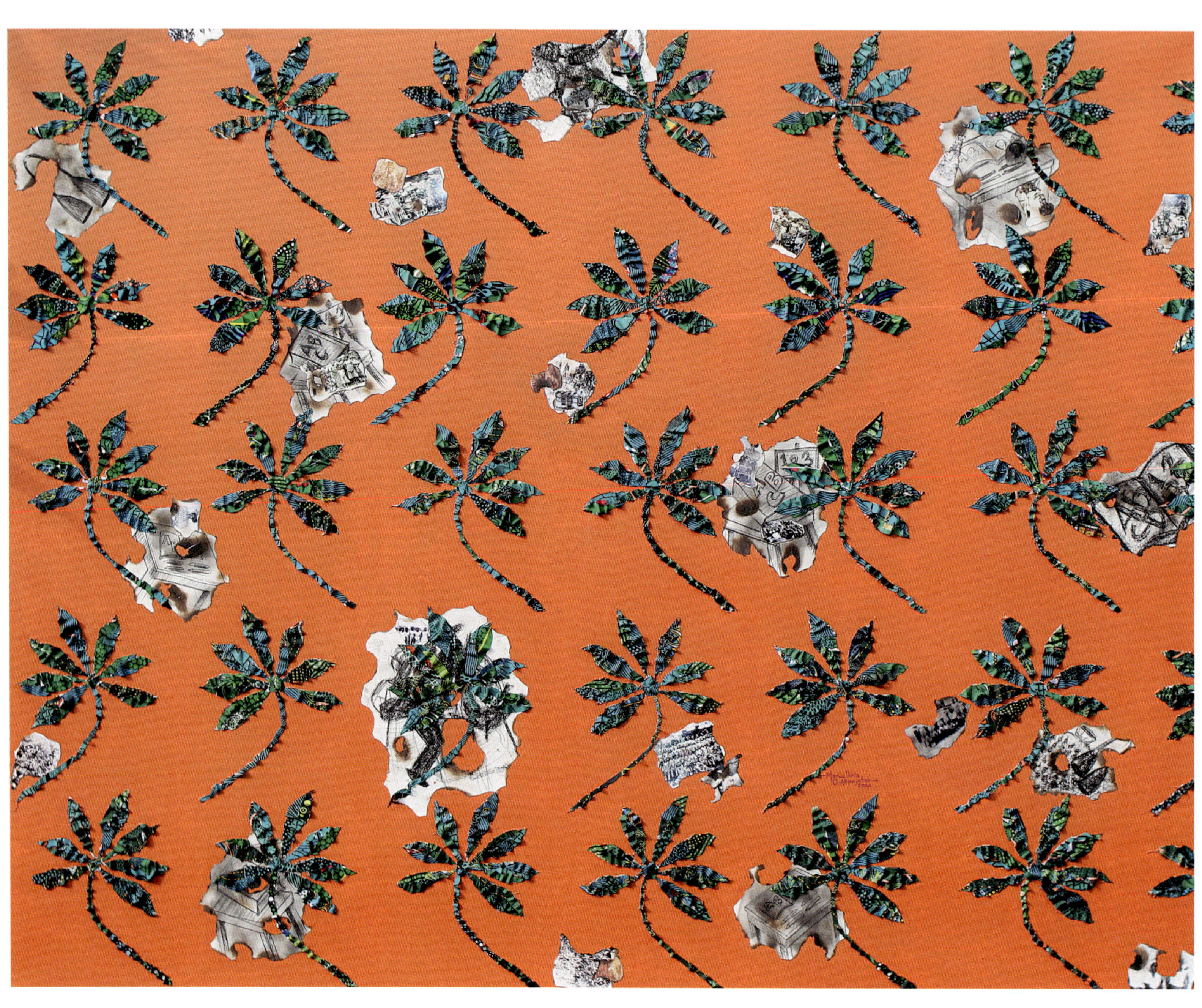

Dreams in Bobozi Farm I, 2020,
fabric, paper and acrylic on canvas,
48 × 60 in.

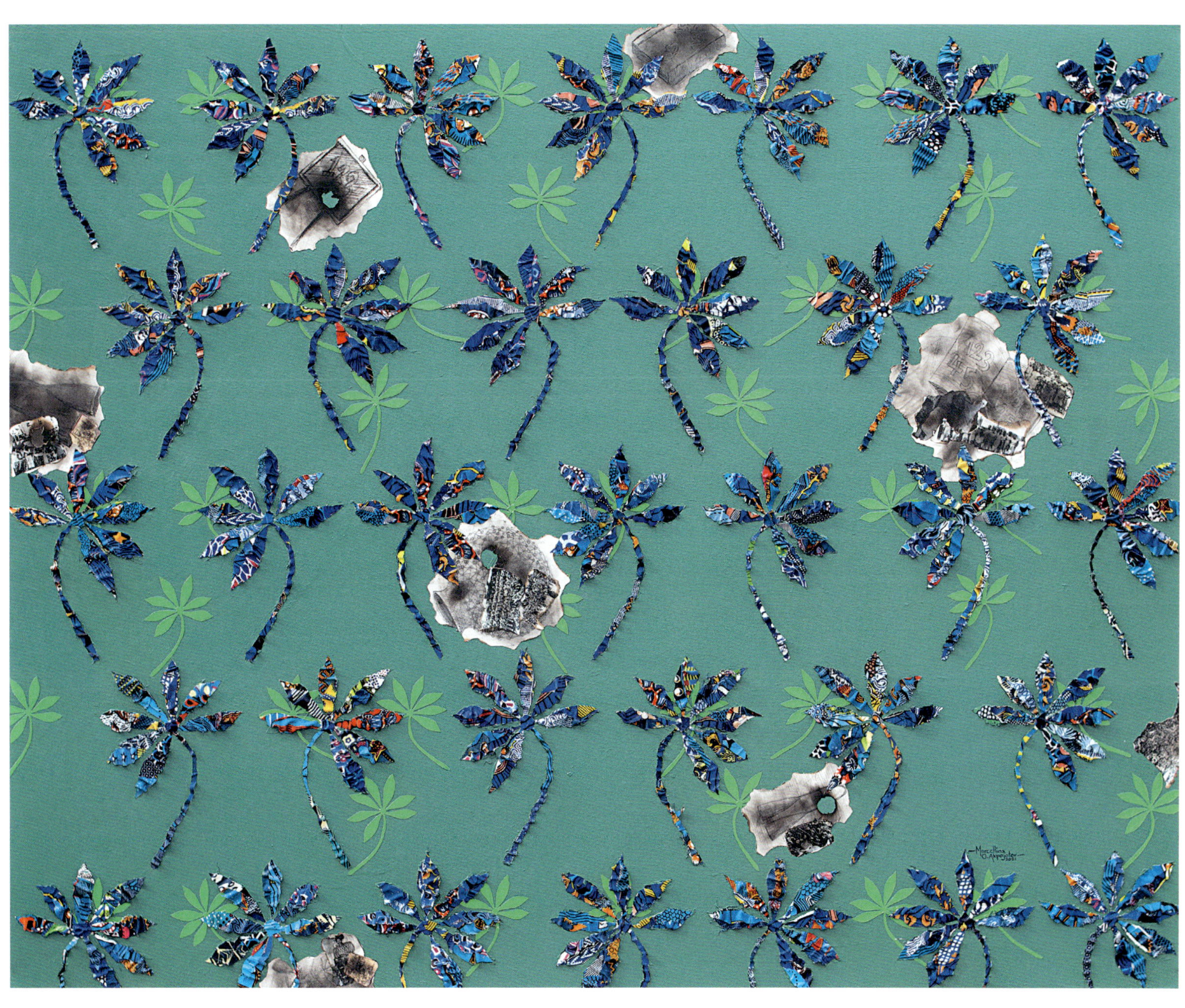

Dreams in Bobozi Farm III, 2021,
fabric, paper and acrylic on canvas,
48 × 60 in.

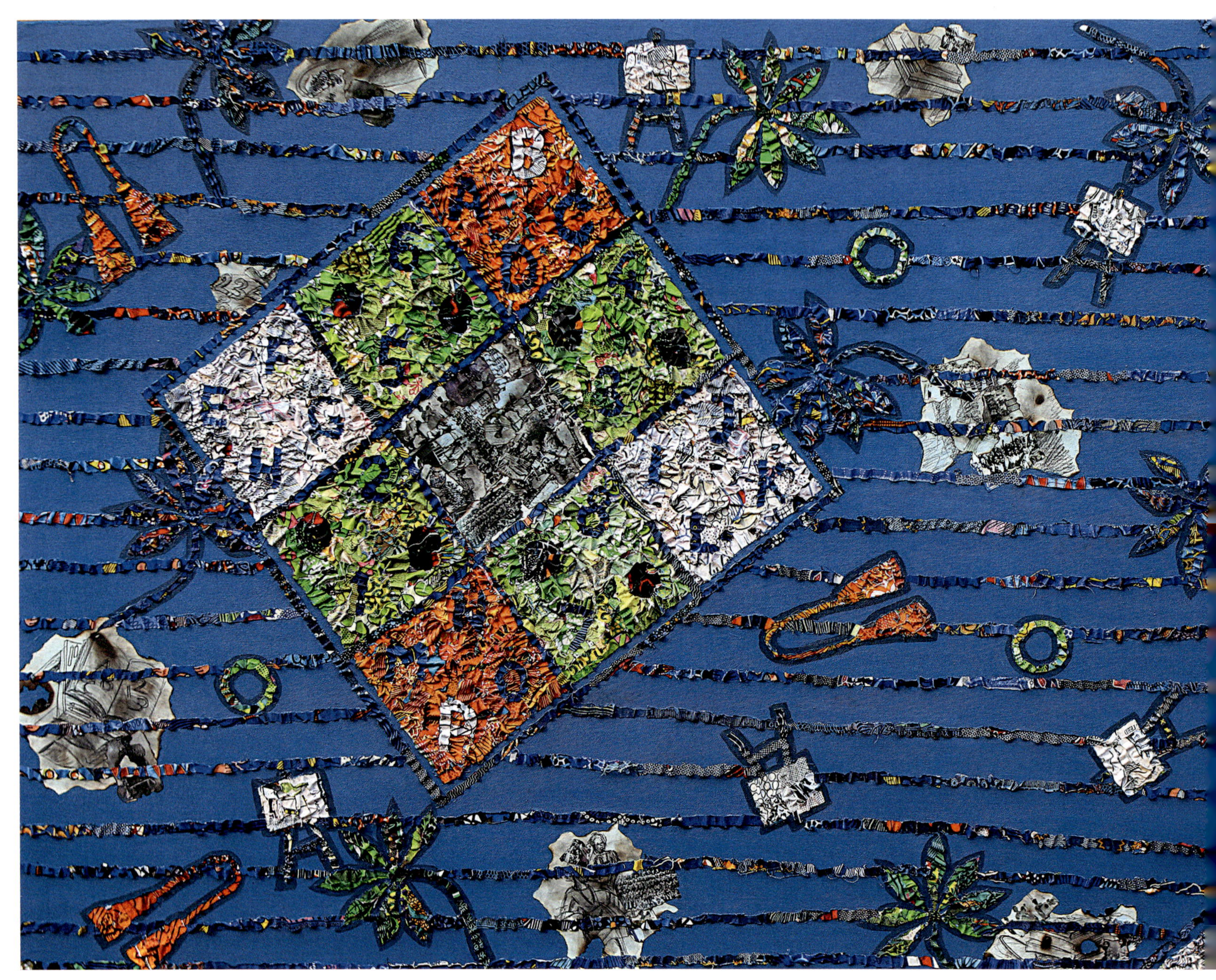

Quest for Education I, 2020,
mixed media on canvas,
48 × 72 in.

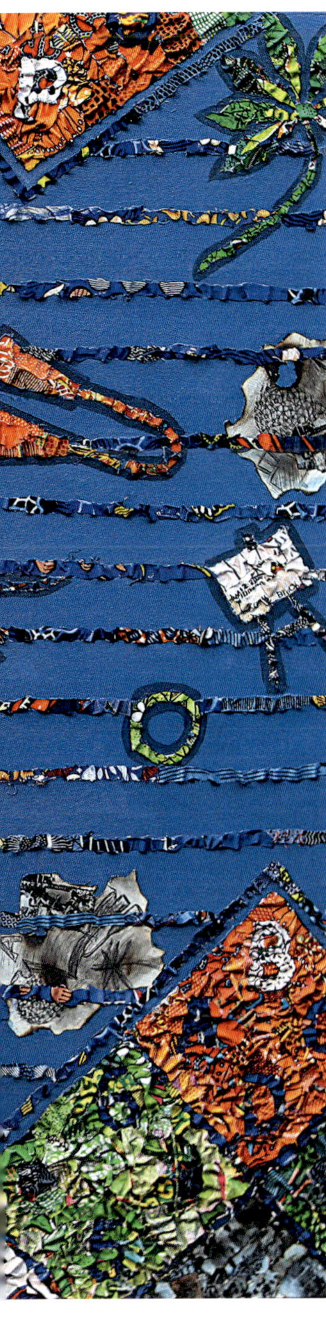

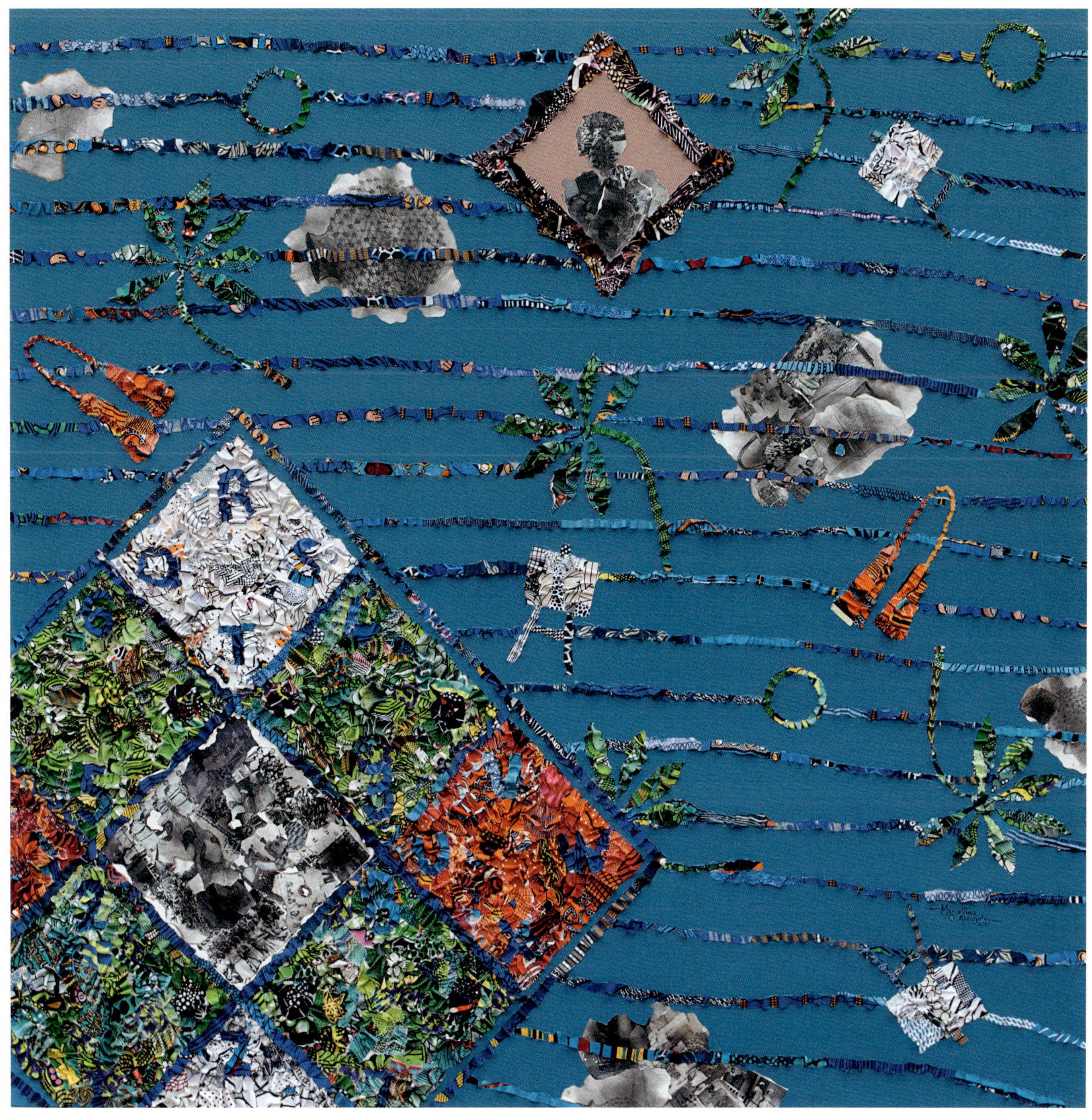

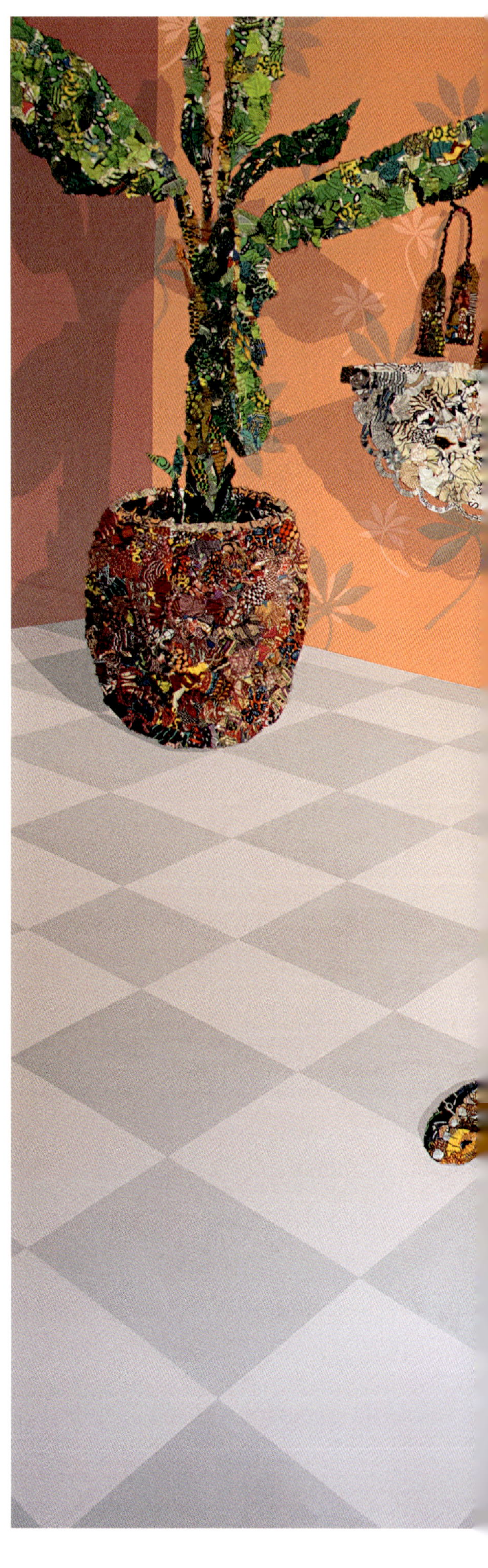

Songs of Home, 2021,
fabric, paper and acrylic on canvas,
96 × 120 in.

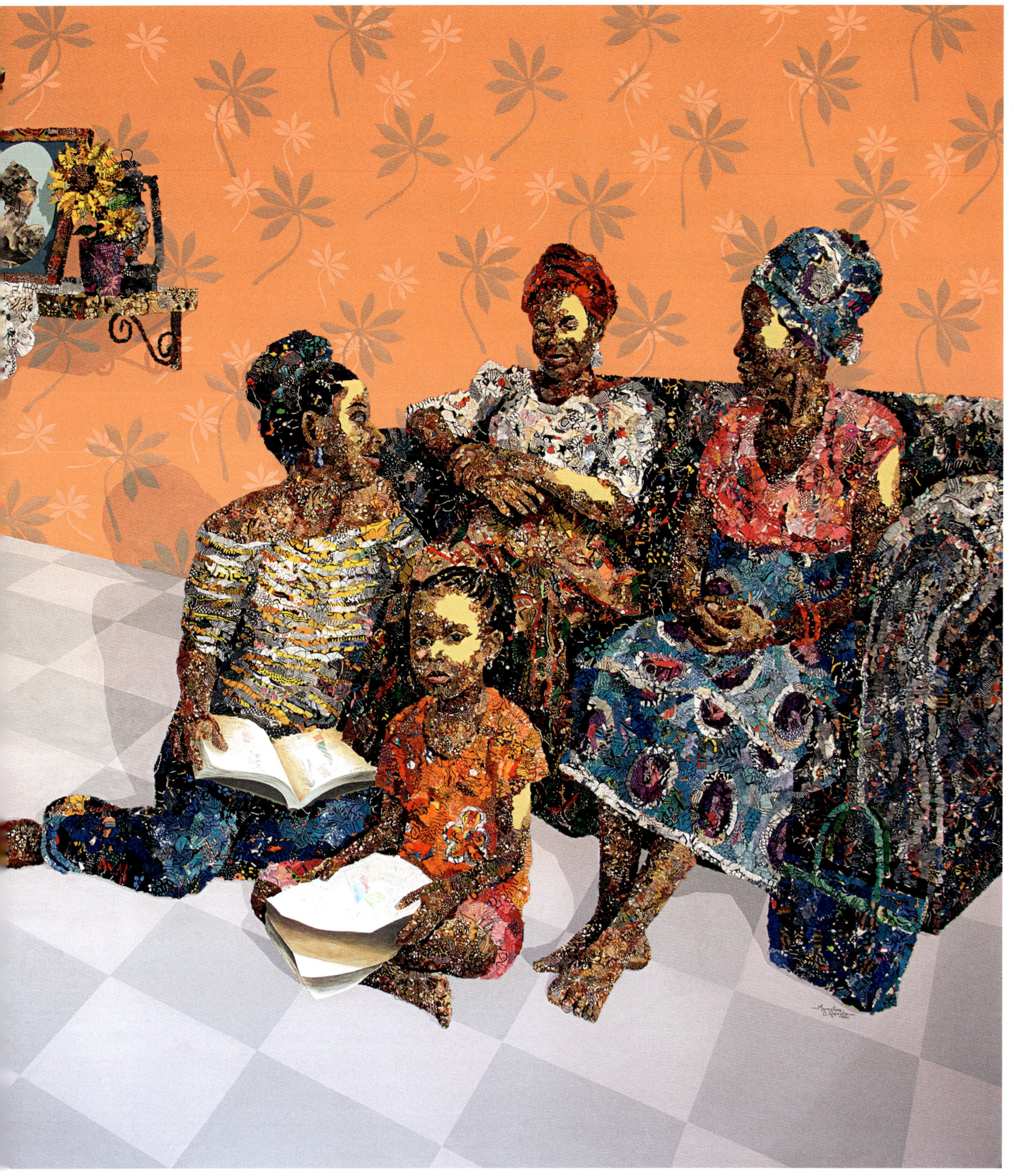

PEARL

This body of work focused on portraits of young girls and women whom the artist encountered at home, schools, workshops and several other places.

Marcellina Akpojotor was fascinated by their faces and the stories embedded within them. By their struggles, vulnerability, joy, beauty and resilient spirit. They are people who inspired the artist or aroused some curiosity.

The artist tried to touch something that is within them. Something that is not immediately apparent. She was also attempting, in a way, to convey their significance and uniqueness.

The pearl is a symbol of feminine power and beauty. It is an ornament that is formed when an irritant like sand enters the oyster's shell. As a way to protect itself, the oyster releases a substance that creates different layers over the irritant until a pearl is formed.

The series celebrates the beauty, joy, glamour, irritation and pain of being a woman, because in spite of all that women go through, they still come out resilient and strong, with splendour and power.

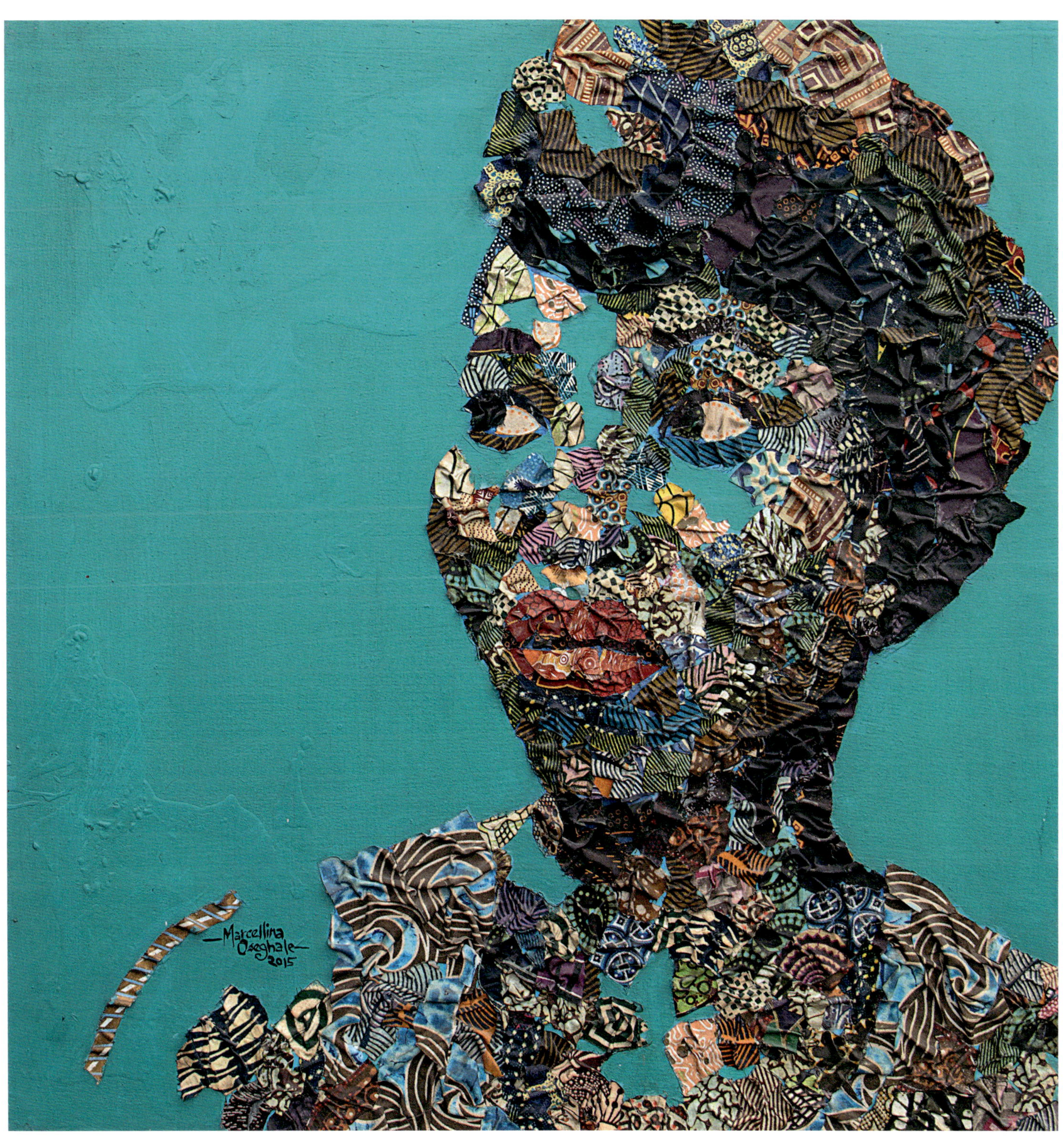

Tobi, 2015,
fabric and acrylic on canvas,
24 × 24 in.

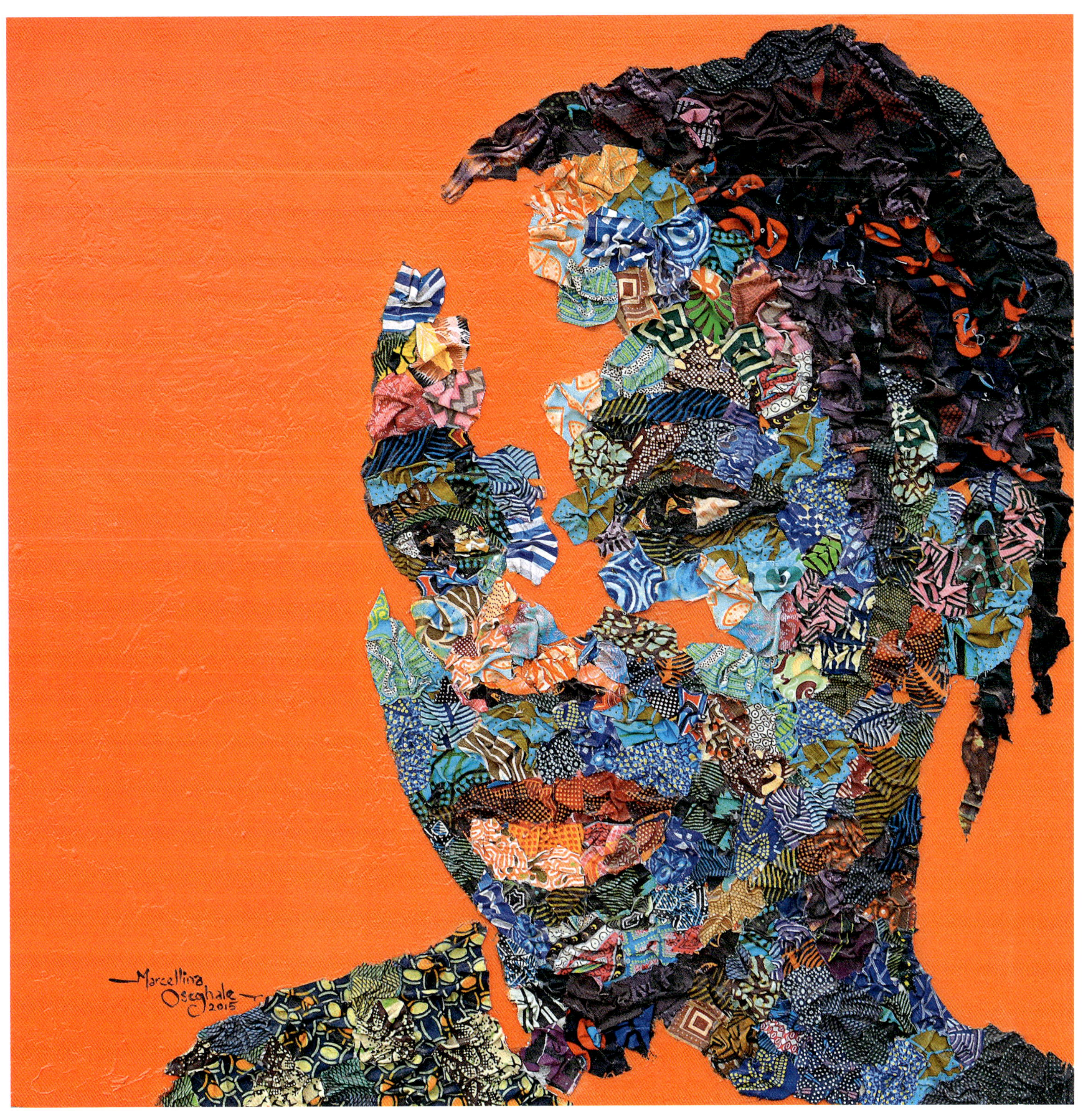

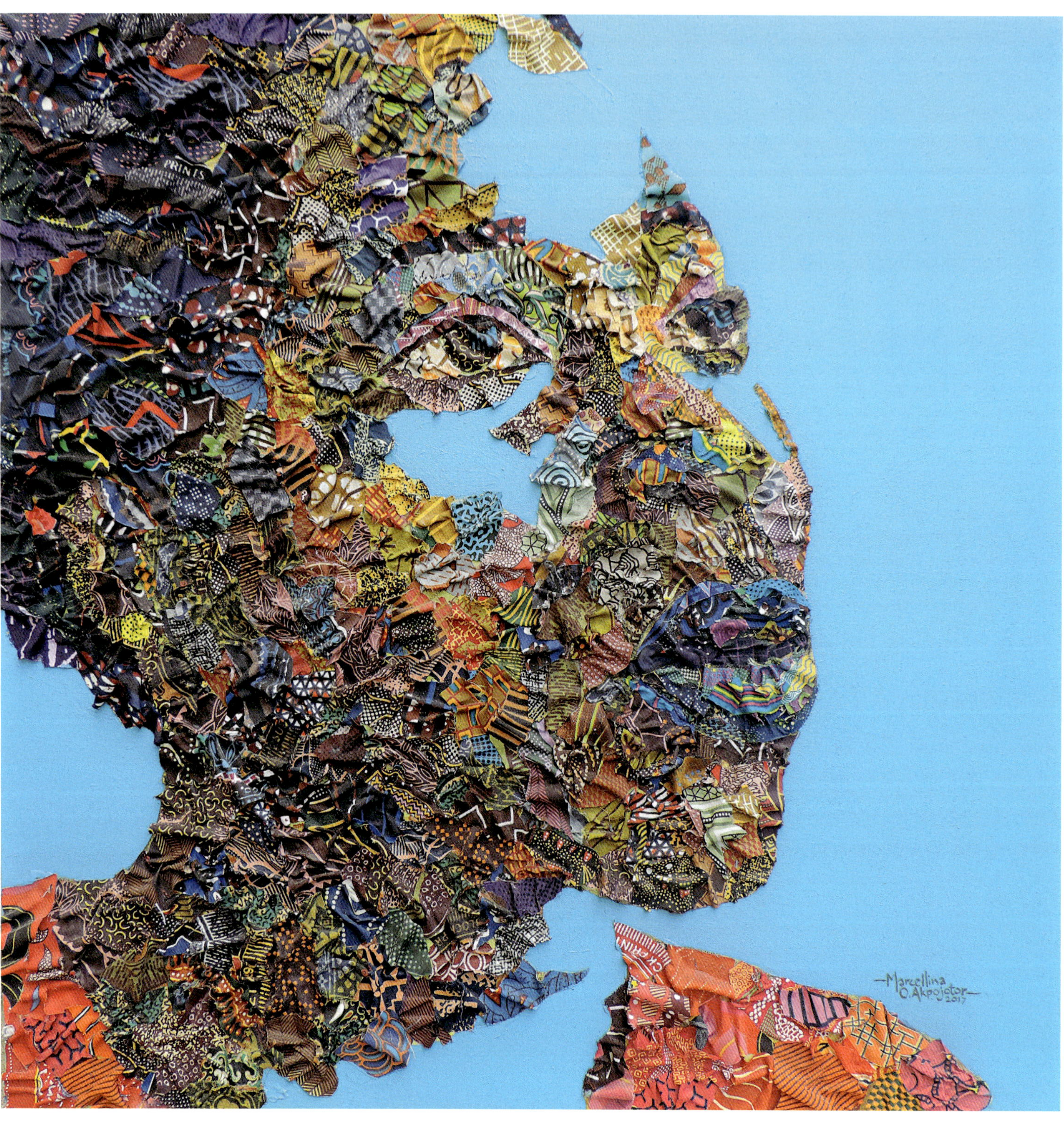

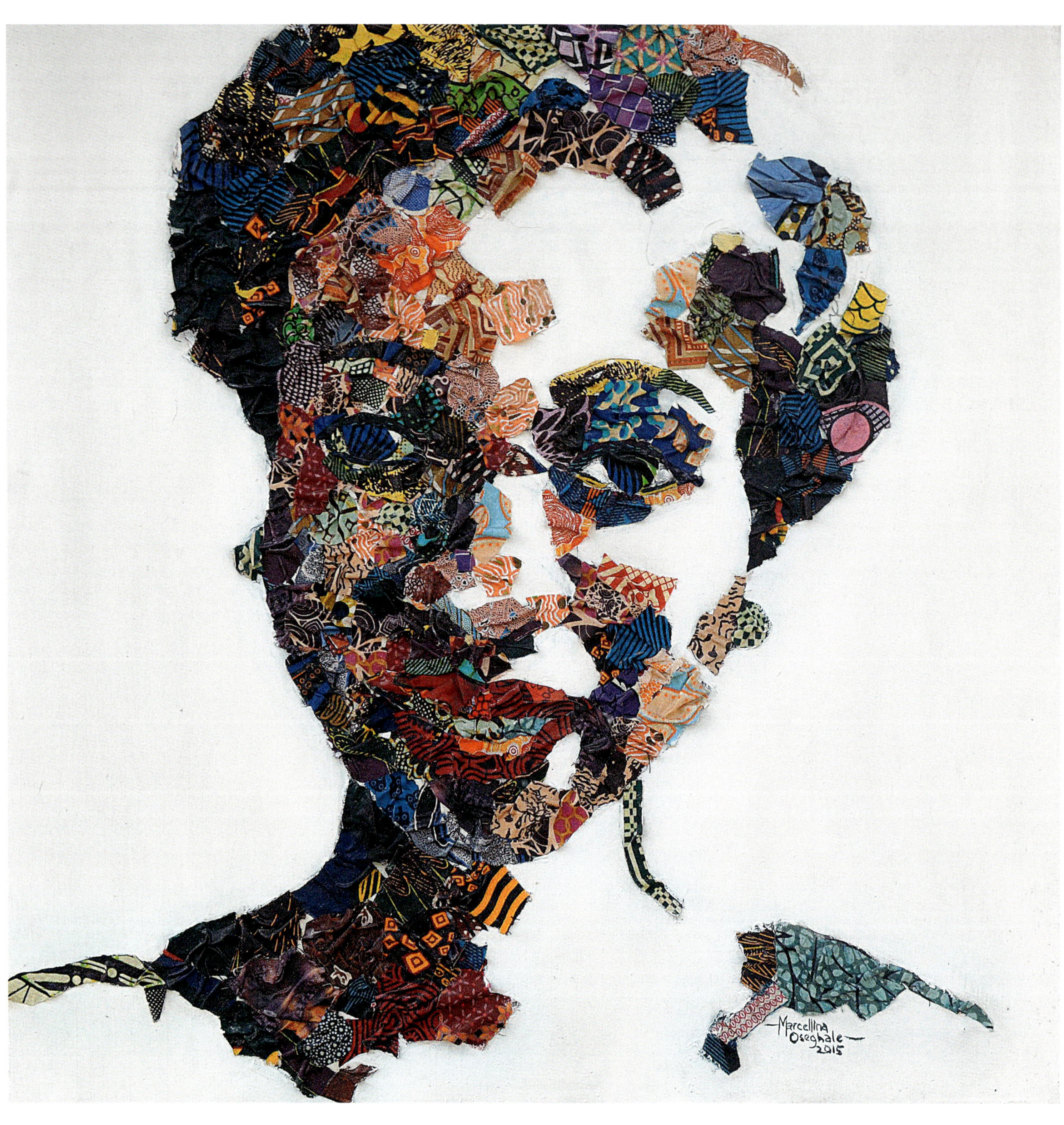

Stella, 2015,
fabric and acrylic on canvas,
24 × 24 in.

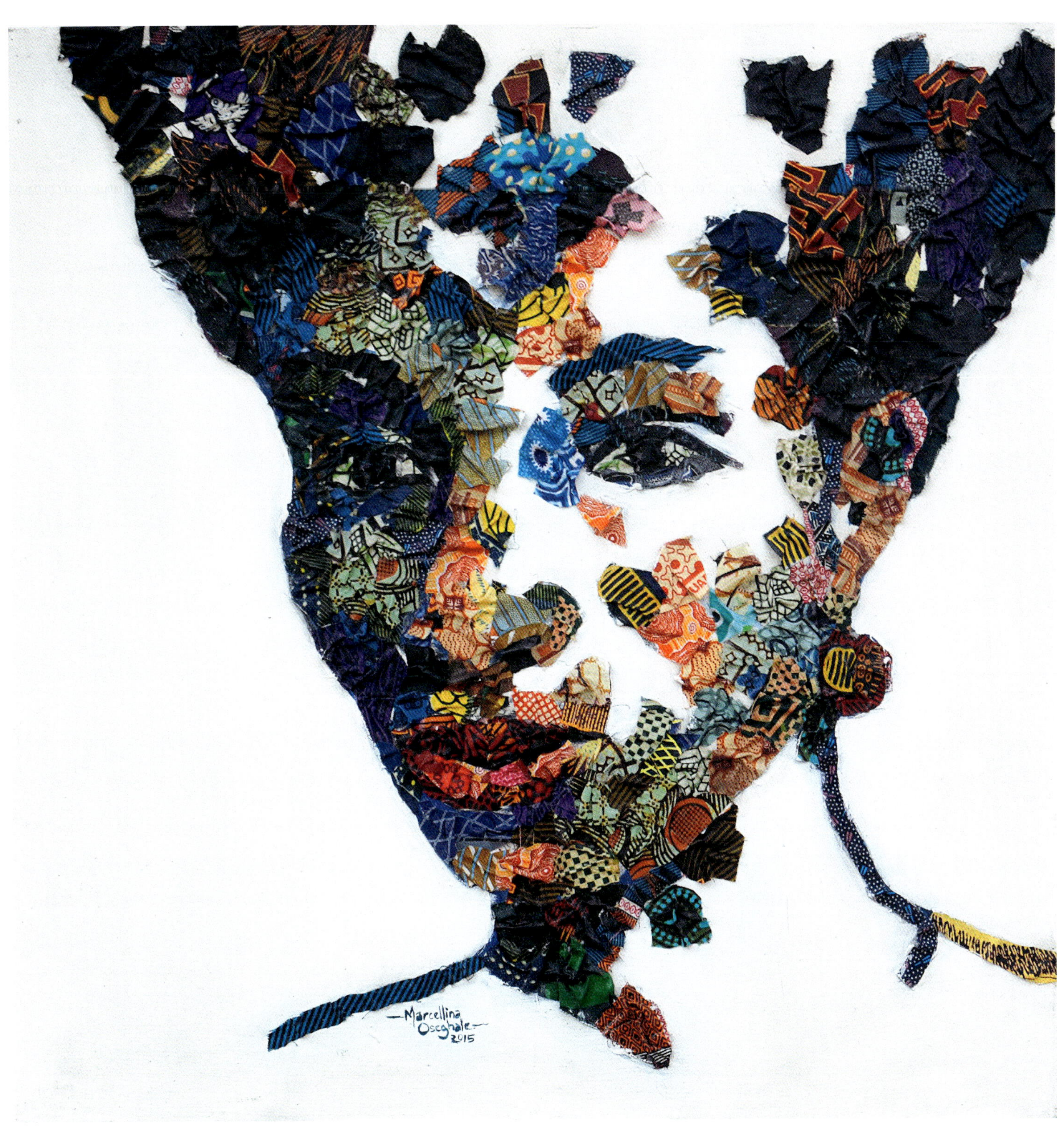

Osas, 2015,
fabric and acrylic on canvas,
24 × 24 in.

Isedua, 2016,
mixed media,
24 × 24 in.

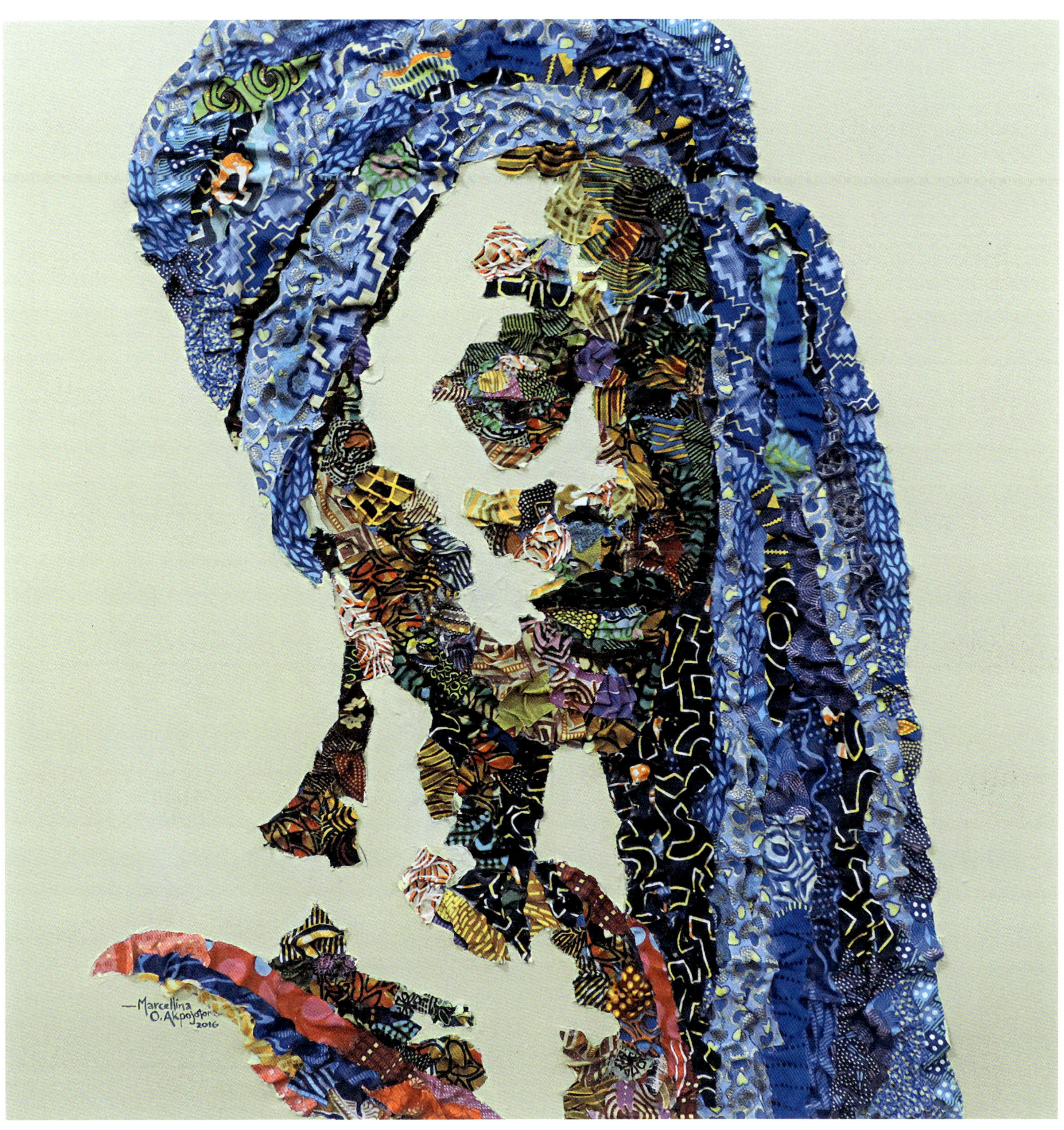
Marcellina
O. Akpoyoro
2016

POWER

Marcellina Akpojotor's 'Power' series is an ode to the countless women all around the world who have found empowerment through education, just as her great-grandmother sought to do with her family.

Her great-grandmother's assertion of knowledge as a key path to liberation inspired this body of work, where Akpojotor portrays strong women, some in elegant, confident poses while some appear to be reading books. In works like *Favourite Spot* and *Good Combo*, Akpojotor intentionally hides the faces of the women as a way to draw the viewer's attention to the book they are holding, thereby emphasising the importance of educating the girl.

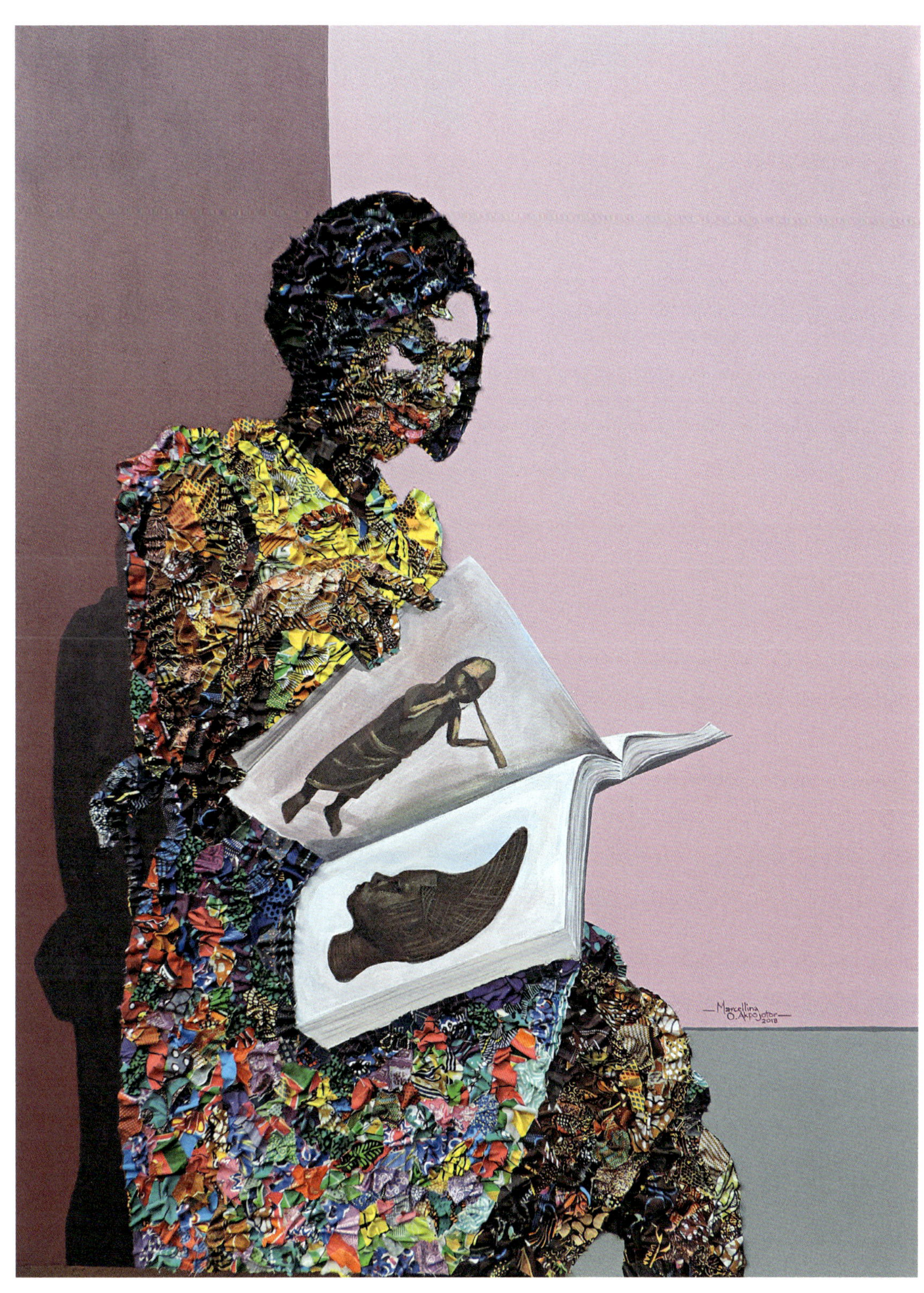

Quest for Ancient Truth, 2018,
mixed media,
36 × 48 in.

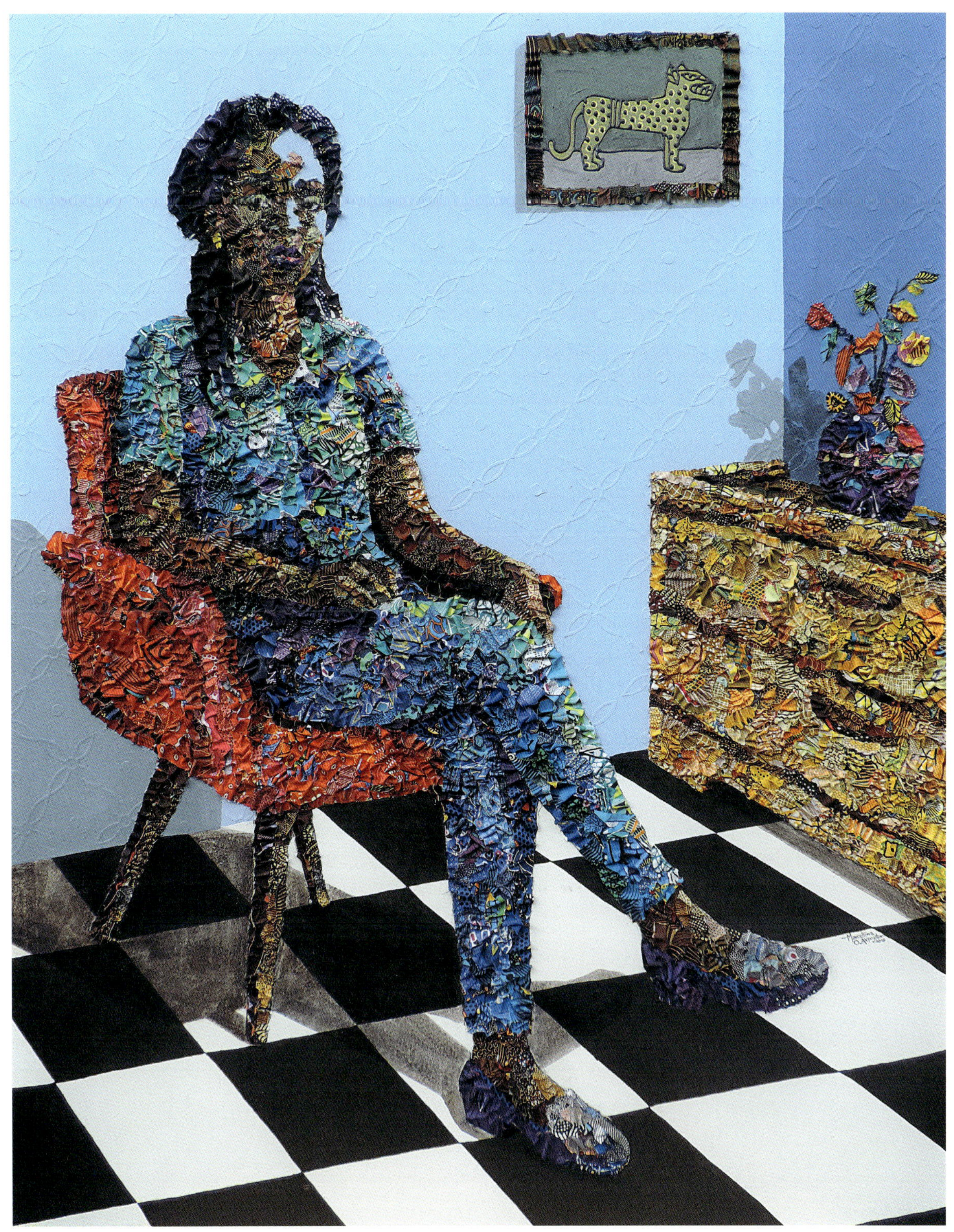

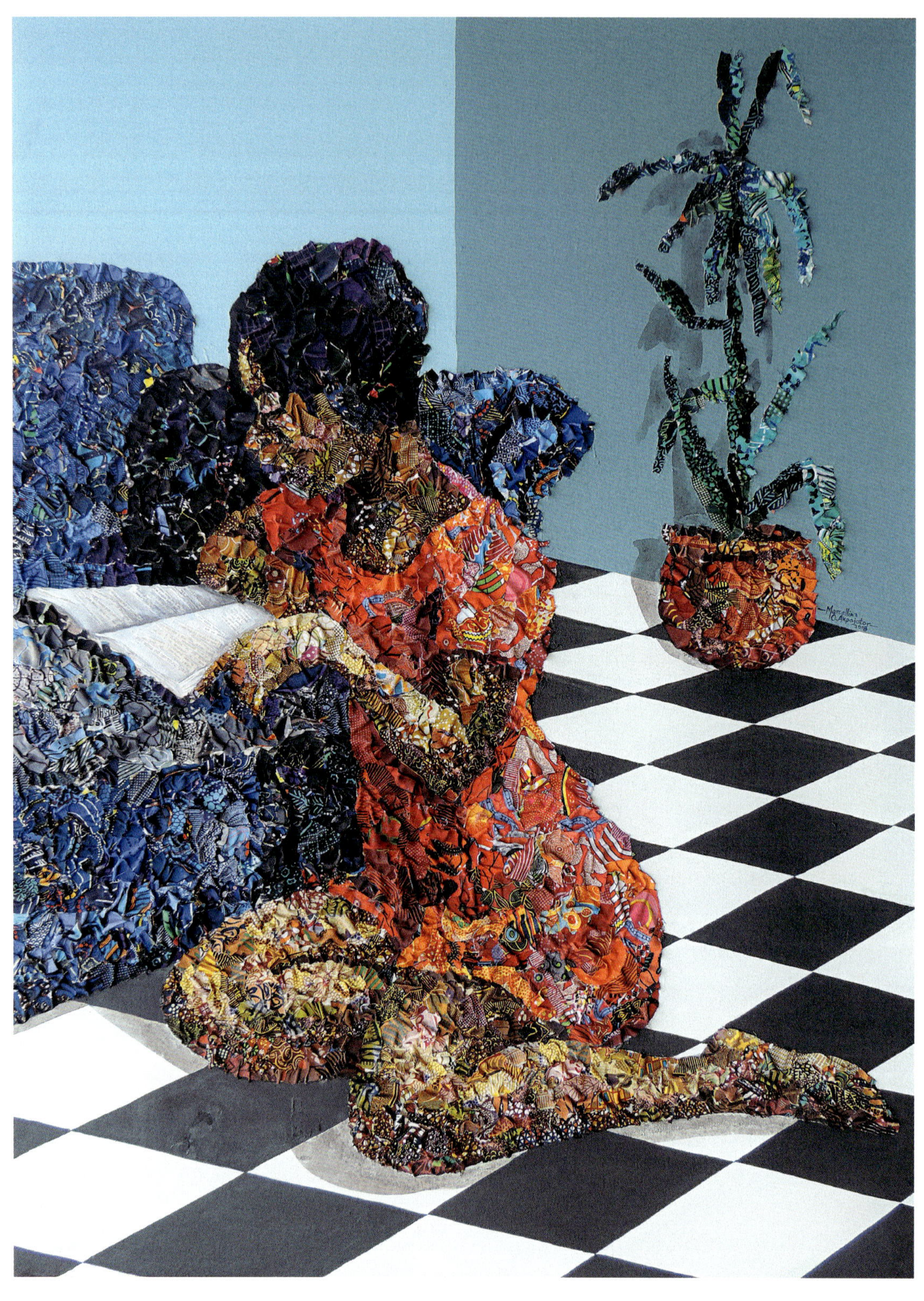

Study Time, 2018,
mixed media,
48 × 36 in.

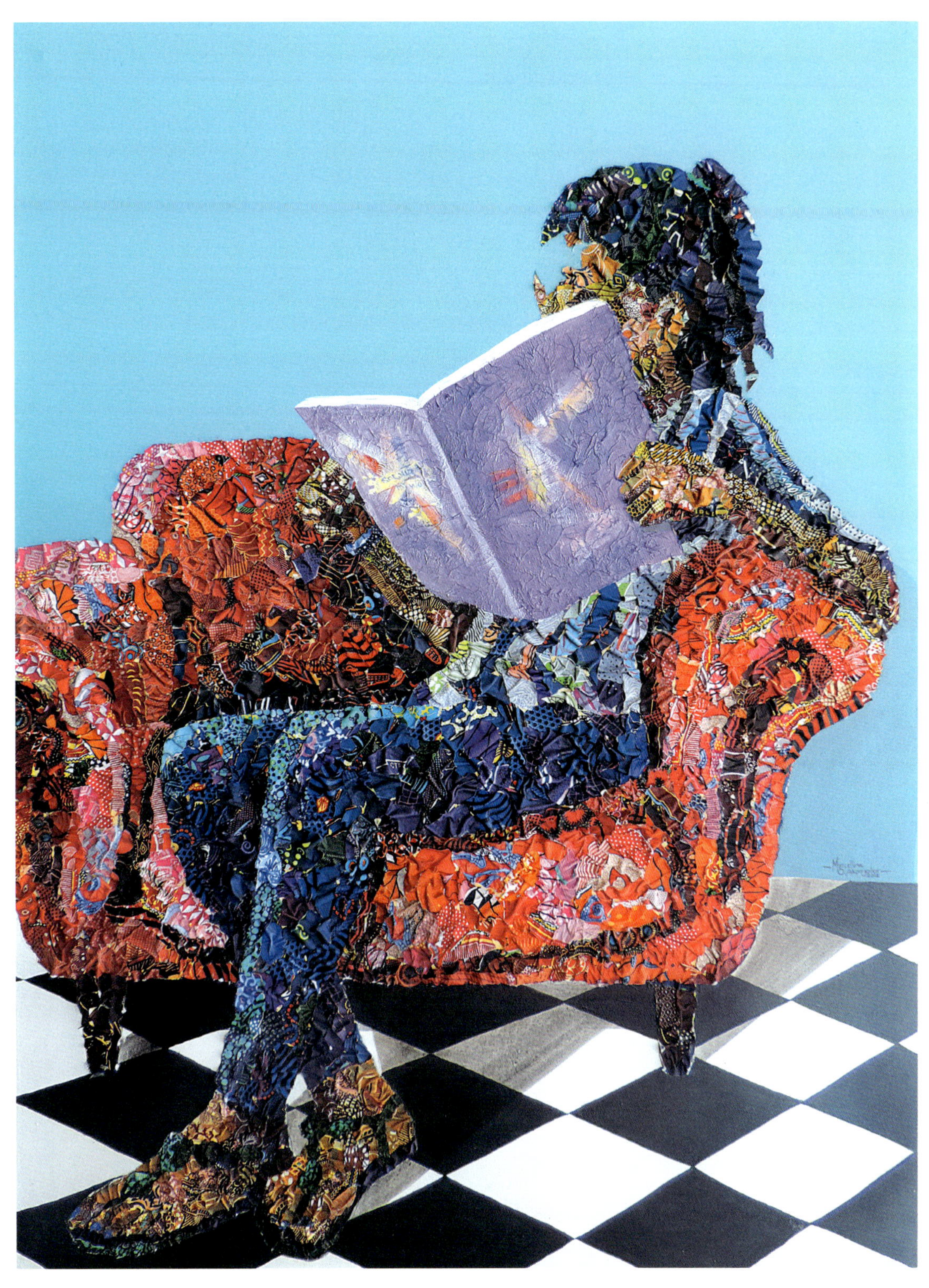

Favourite Spot II, 2018,
mixed media,
48 × 36 in.

Iyanse and Osas, 2018,
mixed media,
48 × 48 in.

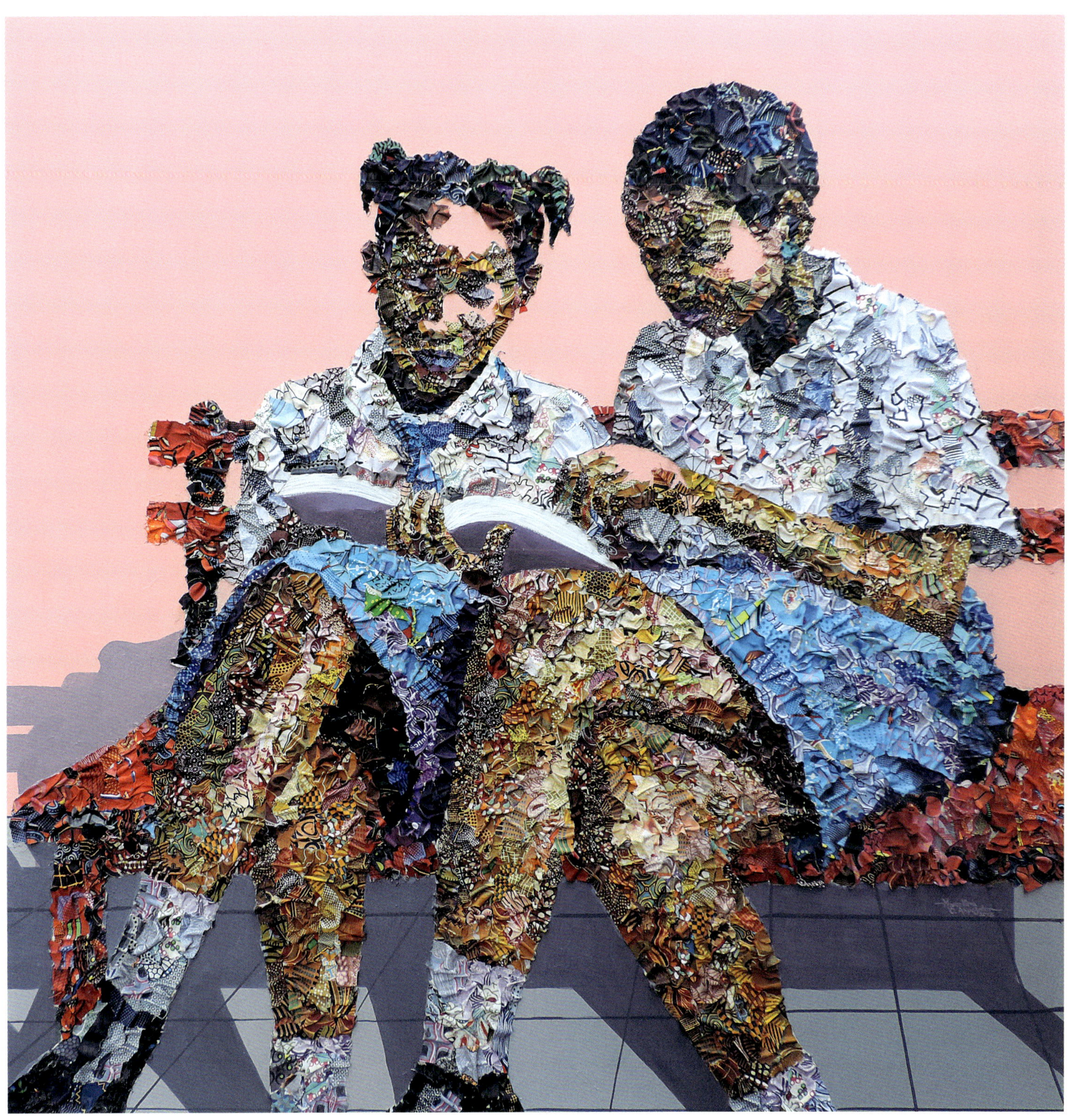

Good Combo, 2018,
mixed media,
36 × 48 in.

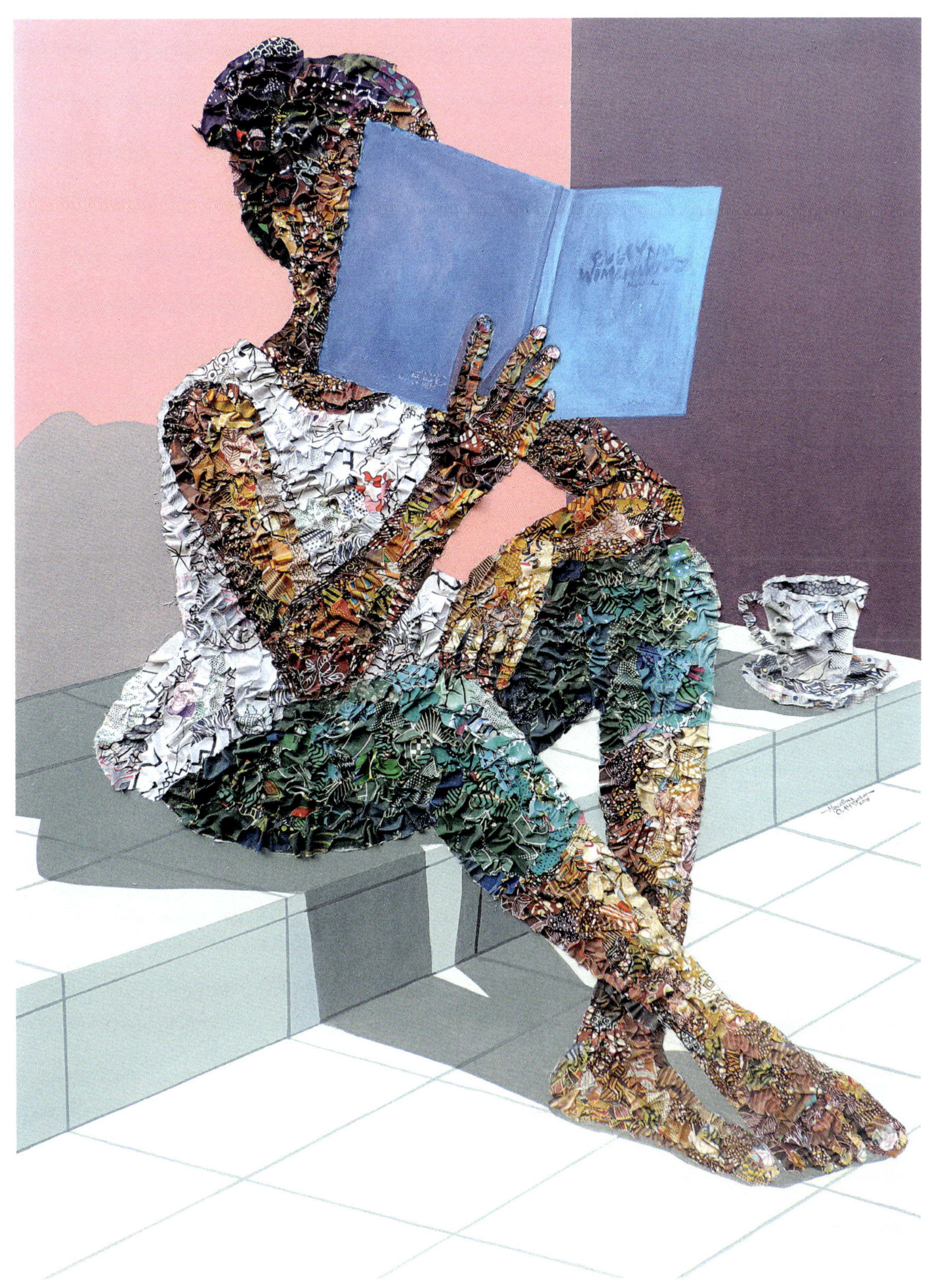

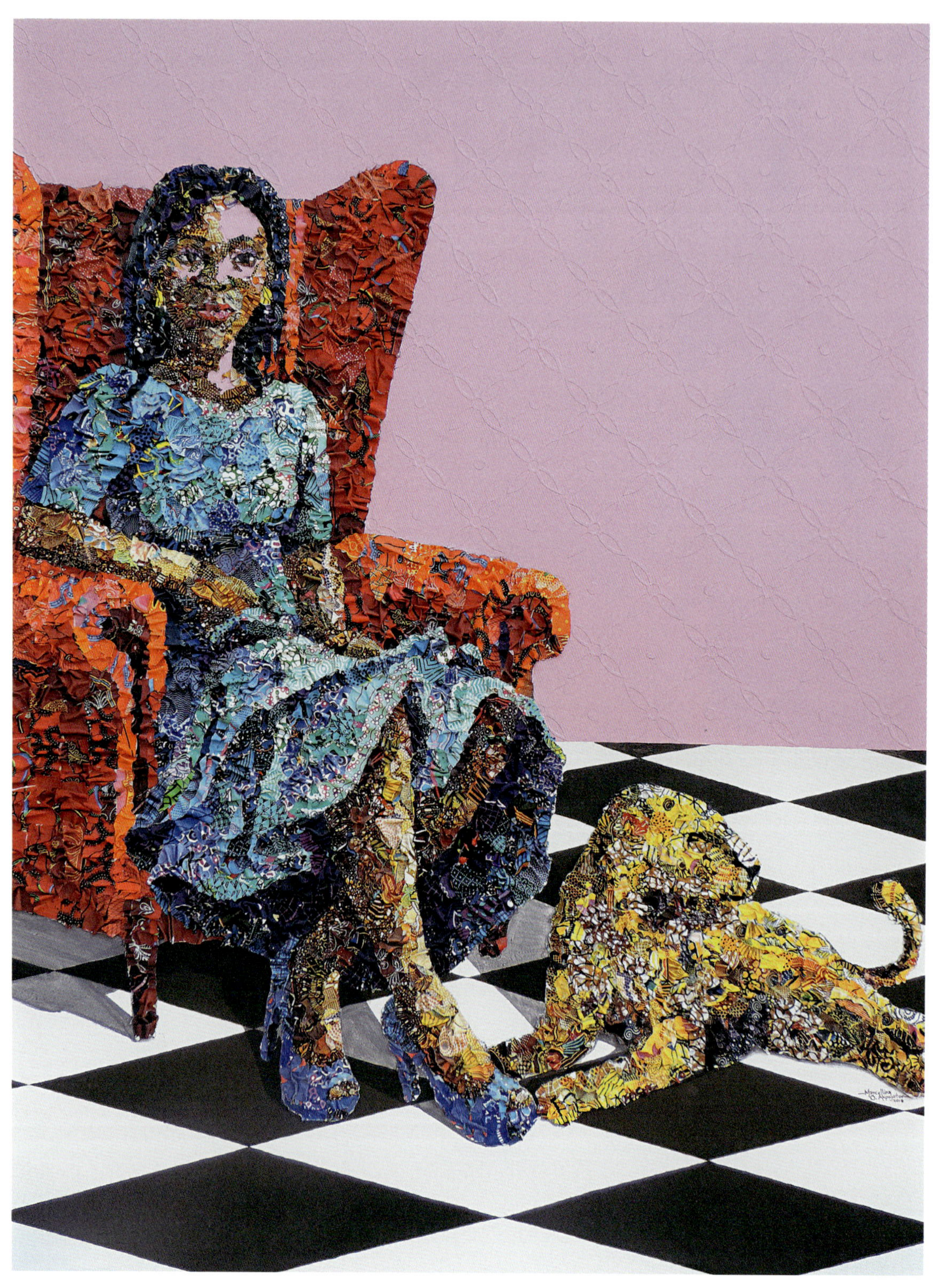

Eyes on the Gold I, 2018,
mixed media,
60 × 48 in.

Favourite Spot, 2018,
mixed media,
48 × 36 in.

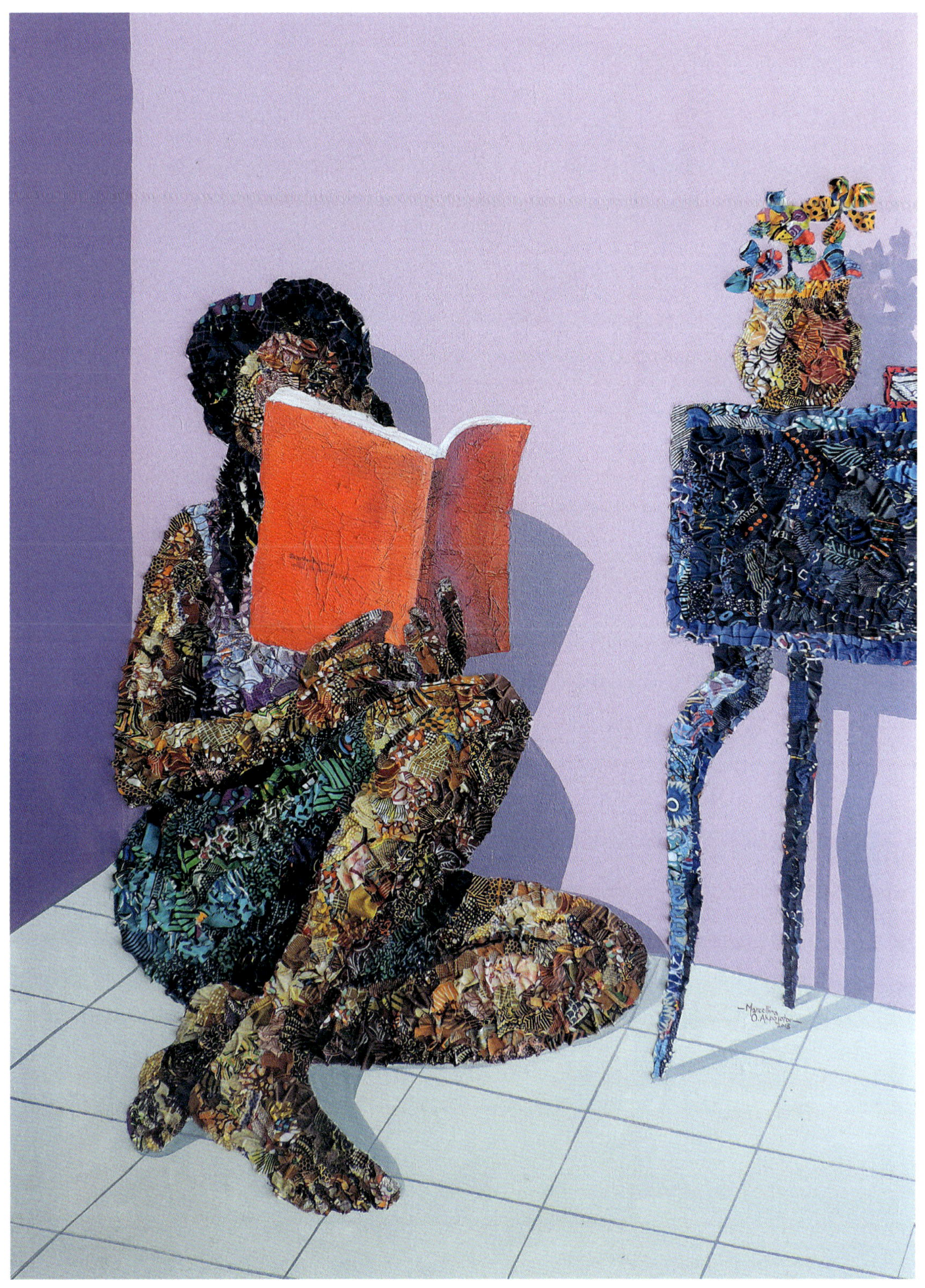

Telling Stories, 2018,
mixed media,
48 × 36 in.

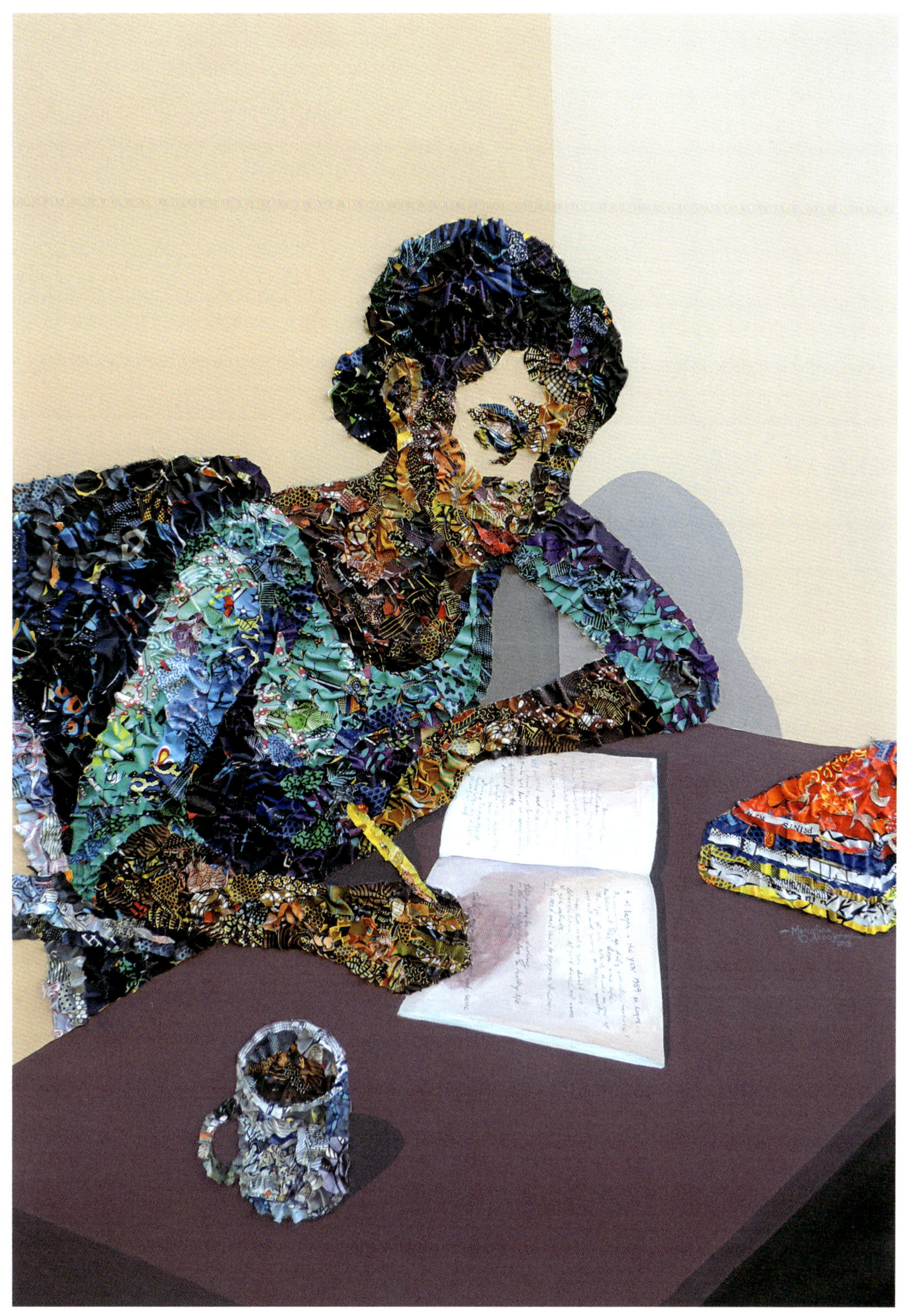

Eyes on the Gold IV, 2018,
mixed media,
60 × 48 in.

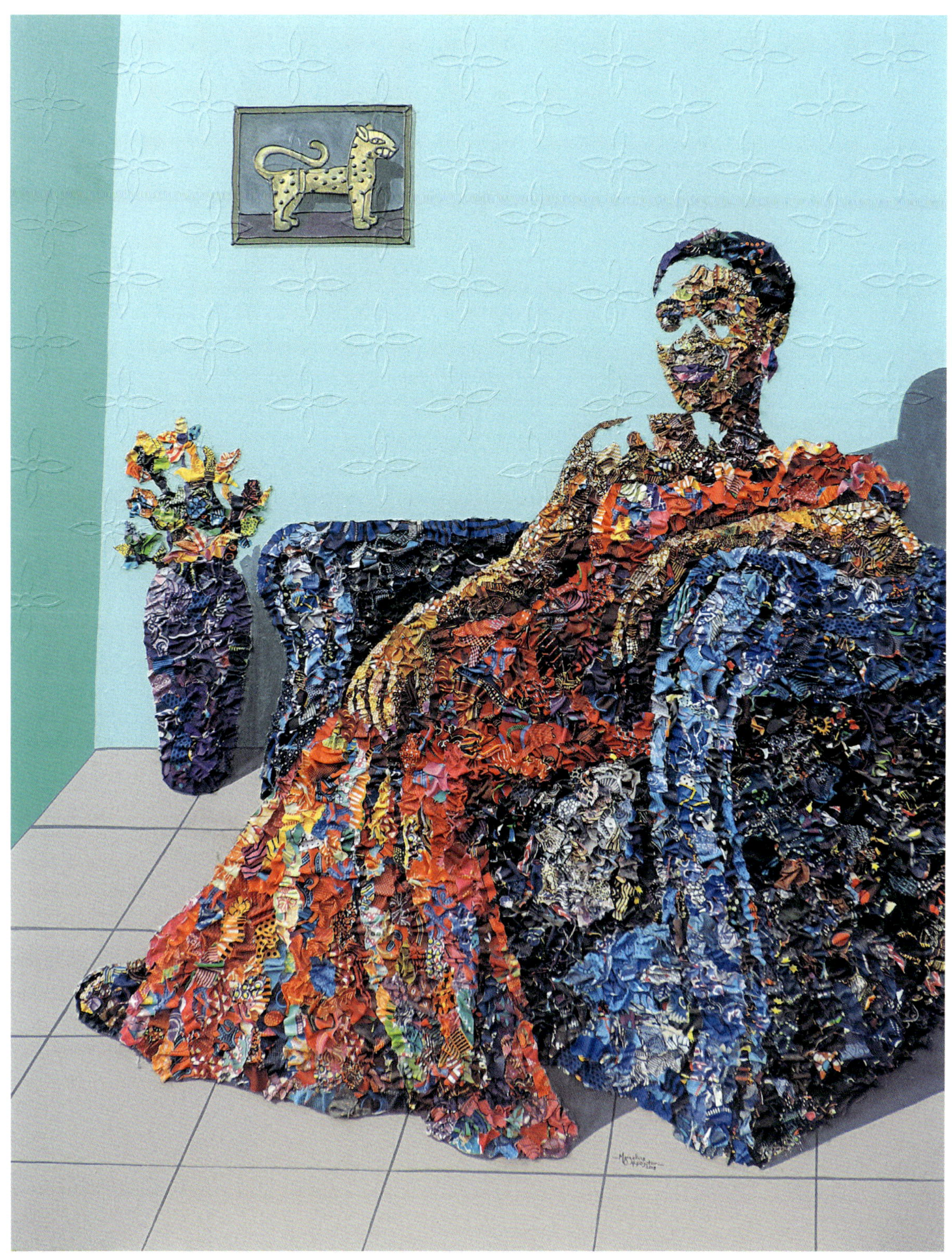

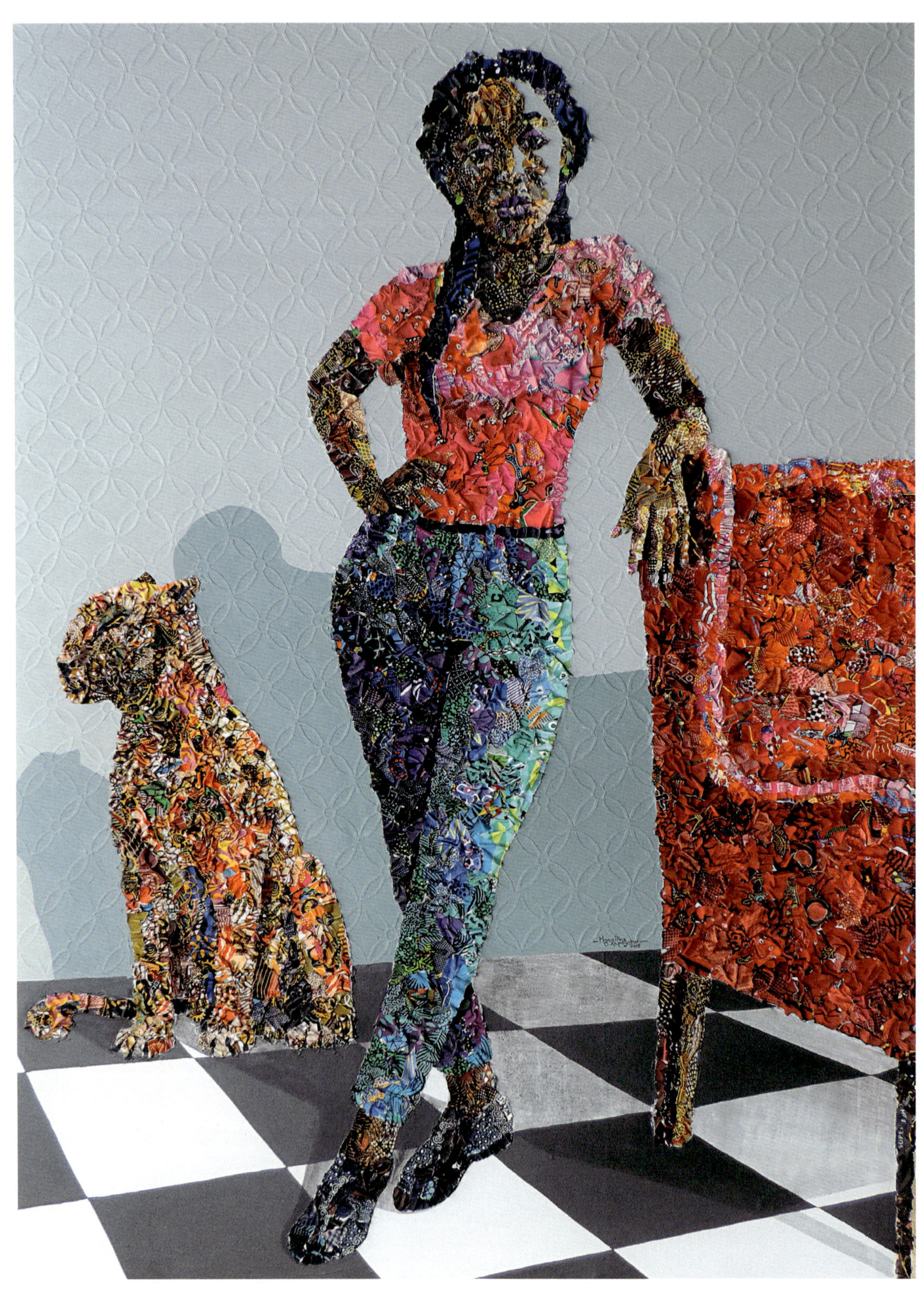

Eyes on the Gold II, 2018,
mixed media,
60 × 48 in.

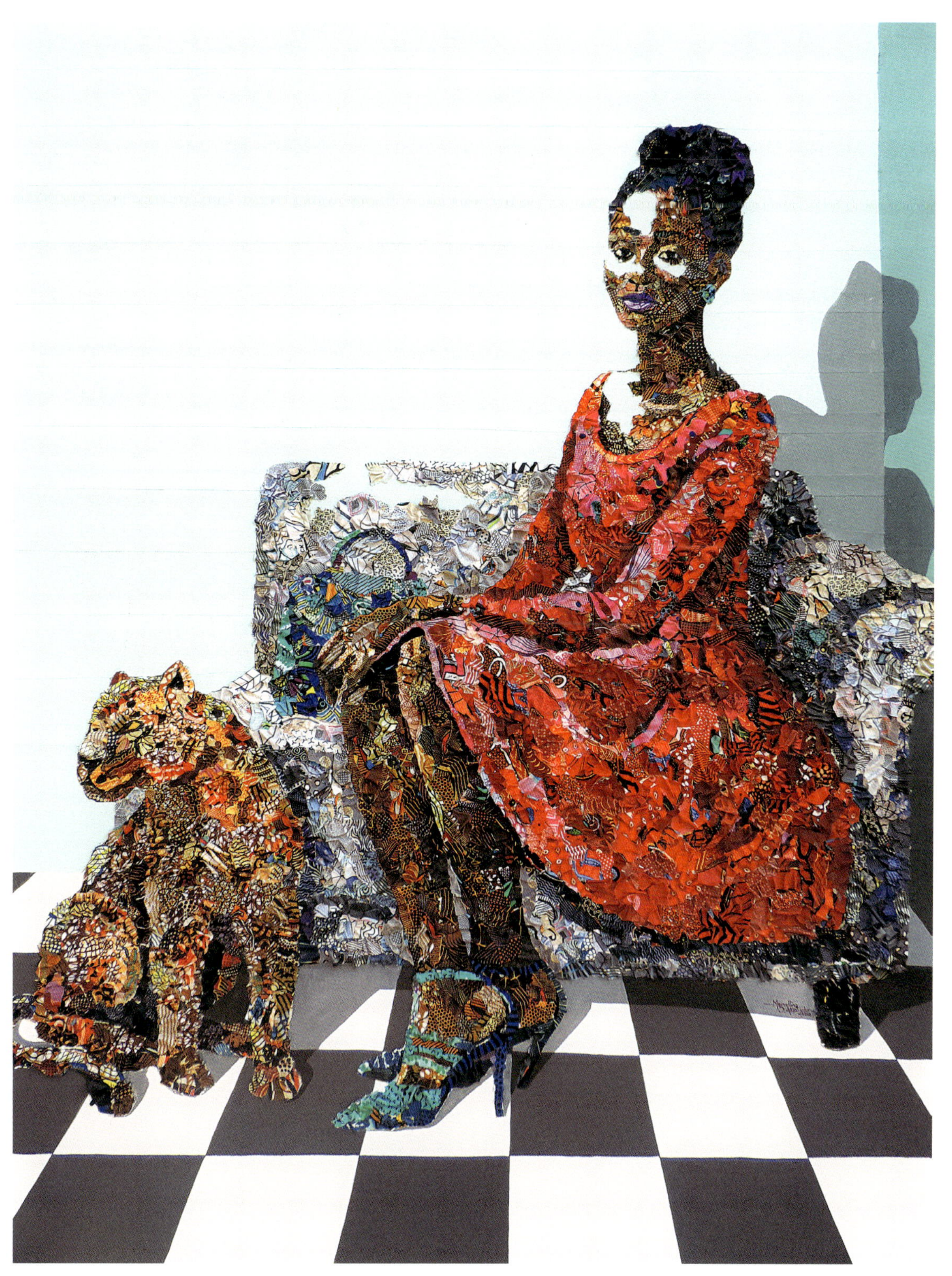

Eyes on the Gold V, 2018,
mixed media,
60 × 48 in.

Eyes on the Gold VI, 2018,
mixed media,
60 × 48 in.

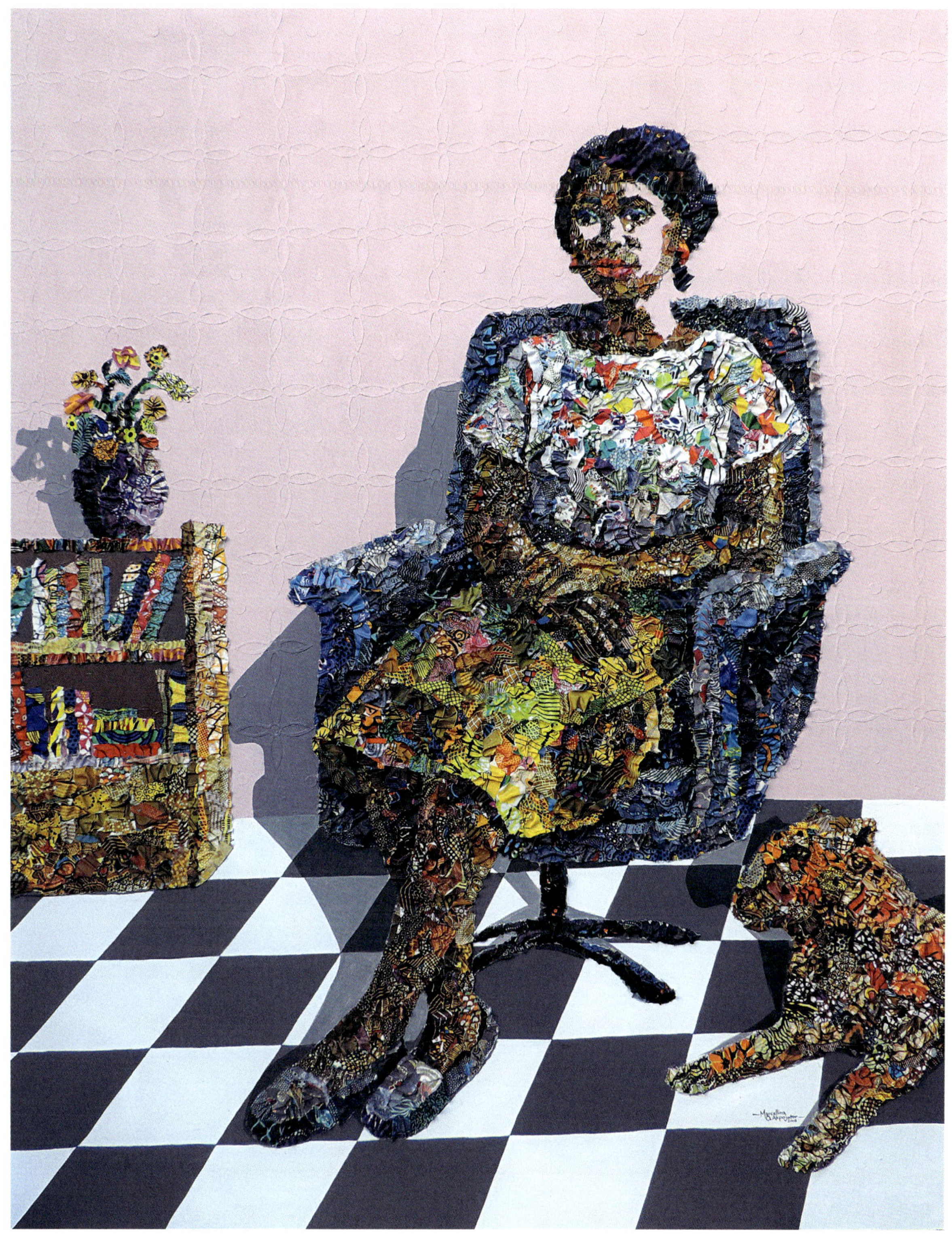

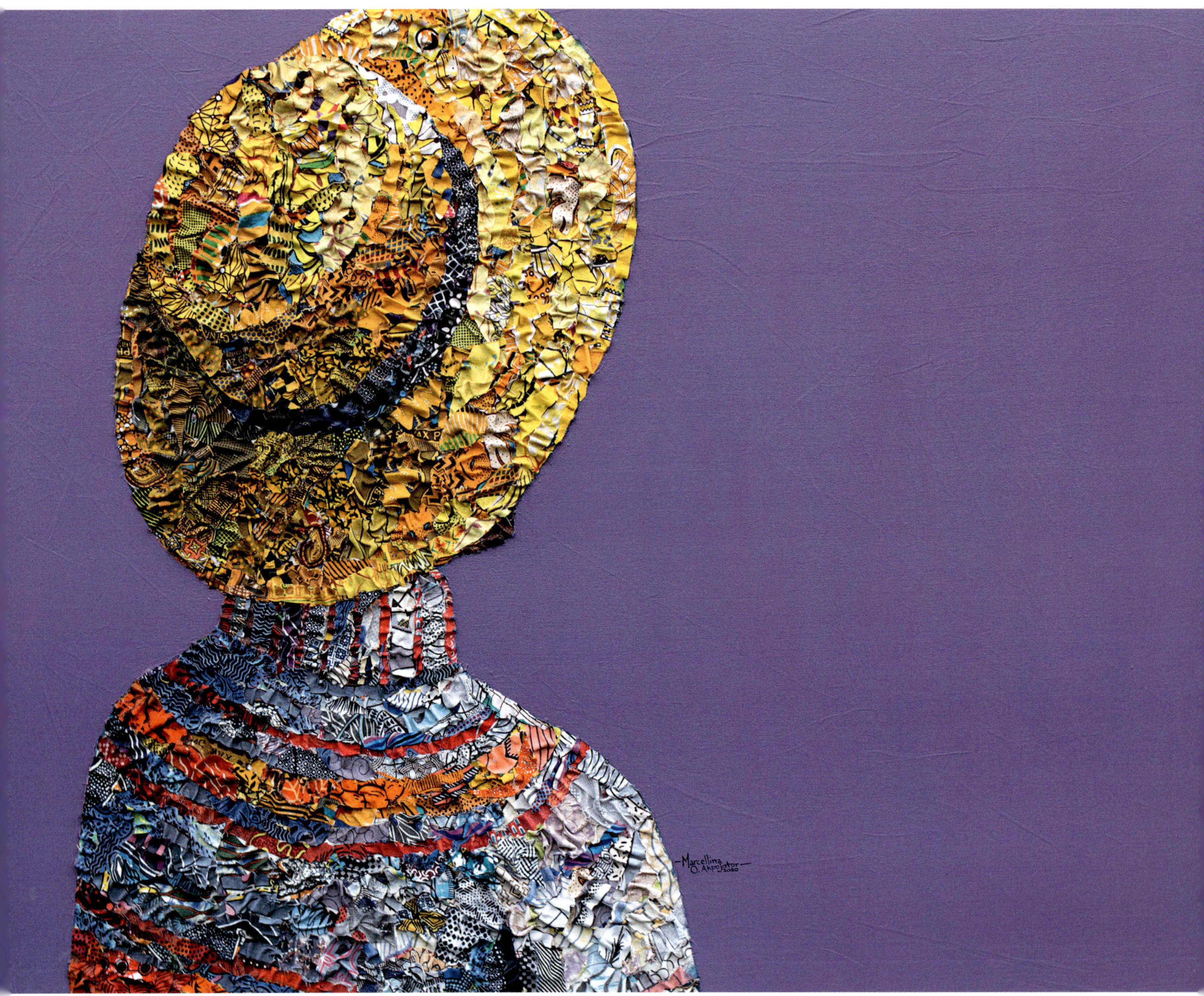

In Conversation with Marcellina Akpojotor

Marcellina Akpojotor – Renée Uba

Renée Uba: Hello Marcellina, thank you for taking the time out to speak with me today. Can you tell me a bit about your art practice and some of the ideas that are important to you in your work?

Marcellina Akpojotor: With my work, I explore women's empowerment, family history and identity; this focus forms the basis of my practice. Within the work, you find snapshots of my family and domestic life, and portraits of women. Over the years, I've been able to use my practice in engaging with five generations of women in my family. Starting from my great-grandmother up to my daughter, my work is created through a generational lens that starts with my great-grandmother.

RU: What practices do you use in exploring your past lineage and how do you gather information about the women in your family? I know you use materials such as photographs, but what other resources do you draw your information from?

MA: A lot of my work draws from listening to stories that are passed down from one generation to another. For example, listening to stories told by my mum about my great-grandmother. It started out with me trying to understand where I come from; understanding the women before me, what they had to go through and how they soldiered on. Then I began to consider my own experiences as well as my daughter's. Due to the fact that I have no memory of my great-grandmother and the absence of photographs, my work delves a bit into abstraction in representing her life. I had to rely on using symbols to narrate some of the experiences of her life.

RU: It's very interesting that you use the cassava plant to represent your great-grandmother. Can you speak about other symbols that come up in your work?

MA: In some of my paintings, you'll see alphabets, numbers and blackboards. With this, I was trying to infuse stories I heard from my mum about my great-grandmother. Stories about how she wanted to be able to go to school but wasn't able to. I think that became a bedrock for the work I do today. This is shown in the 'Power' series, where you find women in different places with books. I know that access to education is a form of empowerment, and when women don't have access to education, they miss out a lot in life. So education symbols became a recurring image in my work.

RU: I know that a lot of your work incorporates the ankara fabric.

MA: Yes, yes.

RU: What inspired you to begin experimenting with ankara?

MA: In 2013 I was making pastel drawings of my siblings' friends when they would come around to play. I had just finished my National Diploma (a two-year programme at the polytechnic), and I was free because it was supposed to be my industrial attachment year. I was making those pastel drawings and also making jewellery from weaving ankara. I became bored after a while and felt like I wasn't pushing myself enough, so

Yellow V, 2020,
fabric and acrylic on canvas,
32 × 42 in.

I was inspired to switch the materials. Instead of using pastels, I started using the fabric itself. Coming from the two-year course at the polytechnic, I noticed that some of my senior colleagues in the Painting Department used all kinds of fabrics to create work; they would paint realistic faces and use mixed media for the body. Seeing that also inspired me. I was also concerned with questioning the materiality of the fabrics I got. That was why I started doing the portraits – just the faces of women around me. I didn't lay the fabric flat because I wanted to complicate the entire image. I believe humans are complex beings and I wanted an image that draws people in and offers more information with every viewing. Each day, you should notice a motif or a pattern, just as how we cannot fully understand a person from the first interaction. I think that's what the work does.

RU: You have to really spend time with your work so all these different elements can come out to you. Is this also why you make them very large-scale?

MA: When I started, the first piece I made was 4 by 5 inches. Then after that, I started doing 2 by 2 feet, and have since then gone much bigger. I feel I'm at a point where I really want the figures to be larger than life, so that's why I started exploring the larger canvases.

RU: They're incredible. As you conceptualise your ideas and what you want to communicate in your work, how do you decide which ones you want to bring to life? As you think about your past and create this dialogue between your lineage and your heritage, how do you decide what's important and needs to be shown?

MA: I think any work an artist spends time creating is important because there are a thousand other things that one could have done. I mostly select images that I'm inspired by. Sometimes I have images on my phone which don't speak to me until later. I might be going through my phone gallery and then find myself spending time with an image and I put it in my favourites. Then I forget about it. Other times, the image might spark something within me and I think it could be something more, then I start. Sometimes I start and don't get to finish, while for others, I spend time building the form and I usually like the outcome. It's a process. I like to take pictures a lot from observing people, but when I'm taking those pictures I'm not really thinking of the work, I'm thinking of that moment. I want to capture these moments just for capturing's sake. Then later on I might feature it in my work.

RU: Okay, that makes sense. You have a collection of images that marinate for some time which you then go back to at different points. Who are some artists that you admire and are inspired by?

MA: Earlier in my career, as a young art student I was very much inspired by Bruce Onobrakpeya, and I happened to intern with him for a while where I got to attend his Harmattan Workshop. I also like the work of Peju Alatise. She was one of the few women in the Nigerian art scene then, and it was inspiring seeing a woman do the work that she does. She is someone I look up to. Those two people were my major inspirations at the start of my career. I also admire the works of Jordan Casteel, Alice Neel, Njideka Akunyili Crosby and Alex Katz.

RU: Would you ever collaborate with another artist to make new work?
MA: I do collaborate with other artists by exhibiting my work alongside theirs. There was a time when I and my husband, Patrick Akpojotor, tried to collaborate on a piece, but we didn't finish it. That's the only collaboration I can say I've done.

RU: That must have been an interesting project. Patrick paints, but you use a mixture of paint and collage in your works.
MA: Yes, yes, but this was actually a sculpture. We kind of married my form and his form together to create a piece.

RU: That sounds really fun and must have been a great bonding experience! With you both being artists, what role would you say that an artist plays in society?
MA: Yes! I think the artist plays an important role. Firstly, artists are the consciousness of society. They are the storyteller of society, deciding what stories are important and what gets to be told. This is what inspired my series 'Kesiena's Diary'. I was trying to get a photograph of my great-grandmother and I couldn't find one. So I began to document her life through her growth, her interaction with the environment, her friends and her relationship with her family. I was trying to create imagery that I believe is going to be publicly owned. I mean, it's going to

be owned by one person, but the images can be found with several other people.

I think artists are important in society. They make the world a better, colourful place. They help us think about things we might not necessarily think of. They help us pause and consider how we see – how we see life, how we see ourselves and our family. They help us connect with our innermost parts that can often get lost in the hustle and bustle of life. I remember at Art Basel, I was taking someone through the body of work made about my great-grandmother and the struggle she had, and then this person started crying. I was shocked because I wasn't expecting that reaction. He told me that during COVID he lost his own grandmother and he couldn't travel back for her burial. I had no idea what the story was going to do, I was just focused on telling it.

RU: That's powerful.
MA: Yeah, he felt something, and I think that's what art does. Sometimes I jokingly say music will get you confessing to things you know nothing about by simply singing the lyrics. That's a very powerful phenomenon.

RU: Yes, and you're making a very important mark that's impacting a lot of people. It's beautiful. Earlier, you shared that you started making small paintings and jewellery, which evolved into you making large-scale figurative and abstract portraits. Over time, how would you say your practice has changed or evolved?
MA: Well, when I initially started they were really just 2-by-2-inch portraits of women, but

with time I've been able to delve more into the narrative of the work. One of the things that changed was the scale, then I went from making faces to making complete figures. This started when I went back to school for my bachelor's degree. We would have live drawing classes where models would come into the studio and we would draw them. That kind of inspired me to look at the human figure wholly instead of just the face and try to see how that could add to the story. So from the portraits, I moved on to full figuration, then I started doing group compositions and paying more attention to my backgrounds. Before 2020 I did a bit of the abstract work that we spoke about earlier.

RU: It sounds like there's been a lot of growth and evolution in your process. Do you have a favourite piece or one that speaks to you more than others?

MA: Yes, one of the works from the 'Daughters of Esan' series, *Daughter of Esan (Fifth Generation)* (Cat. p. 61) – the portrait of the little girl looking at a bookshelf with a globe on it, which is a portrait of my daughter when she was younger. I also like one of the works I showed in LA at Rele, *The Dining Table* (Cat. p. 81), which featured me and my two children at the dining table. The first child was working on her assignment and I was watching over her to make sure she was doing it correctly, while the little one reached out to me. I like that work as well. I also like *Songs of Home* (Cat. p. 96–97) because it brings all the generations together. [A framed picture of] my great-grandmother

was placed high up because she's no longer present and I wanted to represent her absence while still giving a sense of her essence within the room.

RU: And why are those three works your three favourites? The last one you explained, but the first two – what is it about those works that speak to you?

MA: I think the poses, then the books because for me – the books represent a dream that my great-grandmother could not attain, but through her desire it's now a legacy passed down to her offspring. For my daughter, that legacy is in reach for her as she looks at the bookshelf … at the dream that my great-grandmother couldn't attain. For her, it's within reach. I liked the composition and the colours, everything was just working.

RU: It's a very beautiful and powerful piece. Could you talk a little bit about your studio space? What type of things do you keep in your space that keep you inspired? Do you listen to music as you're working?

MA: Yes, when I work, sometimes I listen to music. I listen to podcasts as well, so that when I'm working there's something playing in the background.

RU: And what does your studio practice look like?

MA: I'm in my studio almost every day, maybe except on Sundays. I live where I work. The residence is upstairs while the studio is downstairs. I'm able to easily access the studio and I try to make sure I'm always present in the space to create work. I wake up in the morning, do what I need to do, then resume at the studio.

RU: A lot of studio time, it sounds like. What's the best piece of advice that you've received as an artist?

MA: I've received quite a number and I don't know which would be the best, but I think the ones that come to mind are: 'If you can do one then you can do two, if you can do two then you can do four', 'Make your mistakes quick and grow as an artist' and 'Create bodies of work' – that was Jelili Atiku. He advised that I always work in series. It gives you the opportunity to really dive more into the story. He always said, 'body of work, body of work' so I would remember. That was great advice.

RU: Let's talk a bit about creative blocks. Do you ever have creative blocks, and how do you overcome them or work through them?

MA: What I'm learning with creative blocks is that sometimes we experience them because we reject our own ideas and then get to a point where we can't move again. What I do is just start working and see what comes out of it. While I was struggling with a creative block, I realised that it was because I was rejecting my own ideas. A kind of self-sabotage. So instead of rejecting ideas, I'm learning to push through the block and just start. Also, when I'm in the studio and don't feel like creating, music helps me stay connected.

RU: That's quite a powerful realisation to have regarding the creative blocks. What do you think that your great-grandmother and your grandmother would say about your artwork now? What do you imagine their response might be if they could see your work?

MA: I think if they could see my work, they would be happy. They would be in awe. Just like my mum, who supports me. She usually gets discarded fabrics from her tailor and brings them to me whenever she's coming to visit. I think my great-grandmother, if she were alive … she would be very old of course, but I think she would be very happy. She'd be very pleased that her story has been an inspiration to the work that I make.

RU: Yes, and being able to touch so many lives, too. Is there anywhere that you would like to see your work hung or shown – any institutions?

MA: I don't think I have a single place in mind, but I would like for the works to be shown publicly where more people can see, appreciate and converse with them. I'm happy when more people get to see it.

RU: Can you speak on your process for making the images? Do you do sketches first and then blow it up on to the canvas? Do you do the painting first then apply the fabric? How does that usually come together?

MA: I go out once in a while to get the fabric, although I don't have to do it every time I start a new artwork because I have plenty. I gather unused fabrics from tailors who no longer need them and bring them back to my studio. I also like the idea of going into the community to get pieces of their clothes and pieces of stories that I don't know to create my work. It feels like the community is contributing a piece of its history and energy to my work. It also gives me a wide variety of fabrics that I wouldn't have if I were buying them. I like that part of the process. Once I have an idea I like, I sketch it out and print it to figure out how to make the composition work. Then I transfer it on to the canvas and start the collage by attaching the fabric. Eventually, I reach a stage where I begin painting certain parts and stepping back to take a look. It takes time. Sometimes I use paper and watercolours. It reminds me of working with my dad when I was much younger. He was into signwriting and would use different materials like stamps, stencils and various colours to create impressions on other surfaces. When I do this kind of work, it reminds me of that experience with my dad. Sometimes a particular artwork calls for a back-and-forth process. I might use paper, do stencilling, cut out shapes, paste them on to the canvas, paint, step back and review the piece. That back-and-forth keeps happening and then everything falls into place.

RU: Do you find that making art has an impact on other areas of your life or impacts the way that you operate in life?
MA: I think it does. My process can be very time-consuming and I think it has taught me patience – the ability to take my time with situations and understand. Also, because I'm reserved, the work helps initiate conversation and allows me to share my story. My work then becomes a basis for conversation. Just the way we're having a conversation because of the work I have created.

RU: Yes, a very enjoyable conversation. Do you have a community of fellow artists you're a part of?
MA: Yes, I do, but it's not defined. It's mostly over social media with artists who have shown interest in my work. They've been very supportive. I also support other people whose works I like and admire. It's not a defined community but more of a natural relationship. I also have a community within Rele itself, we support each other.

RU: Do you think social media has played a big role in having your artwork reach different groups of people and demographics?
MA: Yes, it's really helped greatly. I started working with Adenrele Sonariwo through Instagram. She saw my work there and reached out to me. That's how our relationship started. It's also helped create opportunities for me. Through Facebook, C. Ben Bosah and Ronke Ekwensi came across my art, liked it and offered me a fellowship. Social media has greatly benefitted my work, helping it travel far and reach wider audiences. People can see it. Unlike the older generation, who were limited by their physical location, the internet has given us the advantage of connecting with people from all around the world. You're able to connect with different people.

RU: Thank you so much, Marcellina. It has been such a pleasure speaking with you.

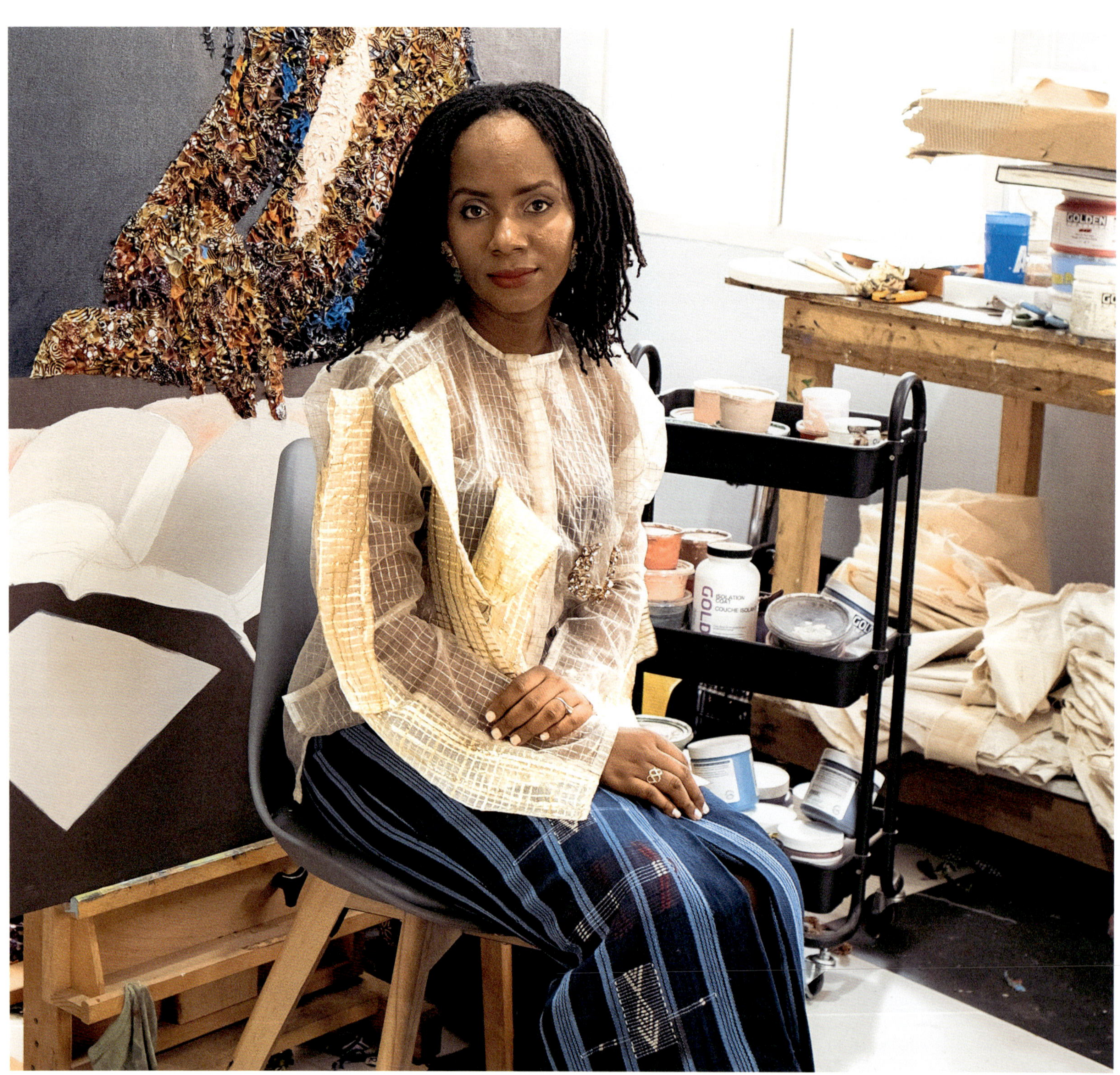

Biography

Born in 1989 in Lagos, Nigeria, Marcellina Akpojotor had her first apprenticeship under her father, assisting him with drawing, design, stencilling, writing and calligraphy work. In 2012, she studied art and industrial design at the Lagos State Polytechnic (National Diploma) before eventually receiving a BA in Fine and Applied Arts from Obafemi Awolowo University, Osun State.

Employing collaging and traditional painting techniques, Akpojotor produces richly textured and layered work with compelling visual imagery exploring femininity, personal and societal identity, and women's empowerment in contemporary society. Working primarily with discarded pieces of ankara fabric (sourced from local fashion houses), commonly known as 'African-print fabric' despite its Dutch origin, she investigates the politics of the fabric as a cultural signifier and a conduit for memory and shared energy. In 2016, she was selected to be a 2017 Rele Arts Foundation Young Contemporary. She was later awarded the Ronke Ekwensi Salon Fellowship following her profile in the publication *The Art of Nigerian Women*, published by Ben Bosah.

Akpojotor has also taken part in several group exhibitions, including *The Flower Show* (2023) at L.A. Louver in Los Angeles; *Narrative as Reality: Constructing an Identity* (2023) at the Martin Museum of Art in Texas; *From Lagos to Seoul* (2022) at VODA Gallery in Seoul, Korea ; *Orita Meta* (2021) at Rele in Los Angeles and; *The Art of Nigerian Women* (2018) at the Carnegie Gallery in Ohio.

Marcellina Akpojotor held her first exhibition, *She Was Not Dreaming* (2018) at Rele in Lagos, and her second, *Daughters of Esan: The Alpha Generation* (2021), at Rele in Los Angeles. Her third solo exhibition, Joy of More Worlds (2024), will be held at Rele in London. She has participated in prominent art fairs and residencies across the world, including a solo booth at Art Basel Miami Beach (2021) and a Fountainhead Residency in Miami (2021). Her work has been collected by prominent public and private institutions.

Marcellina Akpojotor
in her studio, 2023,
Lagos, Nigeria.

Acknowledgements

Éditions Skira Paris and Rele would like to thank Marcellina Akpojotor
for her invaluable contribution and her commitment throughout
the production of this monograph.

Our gratitude also goes to the authors: Marla C. Berns,
Ugochukwu-Smooth C. Nzewi, Bruce Onobrakpeya and Frank Ugiomoh,
whose texts provide deep insight into the artist's work. We would also
like to thank Renée Uba for her conversation with the artist.

We also extend our sincere thanks to the collectors and the institutions
that have exhibited Marcellina Akpojotor's work while showing her
staunch support.

The artist would like to thank her great-grandmother, Dede Eboheide,
who dared to dream; her husband, Patrick; her daughters, Kesiena and
Amiede; her parents; and all other members of her family, especially for
their support and for being a great source of inspiration.

The artist would also like to thank her studio assistants both past and
present: Michelle Okpare, Joseph Idowu, Taiwo Oguntola, Peter Adelaja
and David Oseghale, along with Ayobami Ogungbe, who photographed
her in her studio.

Special thanks go to Adenrele Sonariwo, Rele and the whole team for
making this endeavour a success.

To all, we express our gratitude for their contribution, as well as those
who preferred to remain anonymous.

RELE, LONDON
5–7 Dover Street,
London W1S 4LD

RELE, LAGOS
32 Thompson Avenue,
Ikoyi, Lagos

RELE, LOS ANGELES
711 N Western Avenue,
Los Angeles, CA 90029
https://www.rele.co/

Founding Director
Adenrele Sonariwo

ÉDITIONS SKIRA PARIS
14 rue Serpente
75006 Paris
www.skira.net

Senior Editor
Nathalie Prat-Couadau

Project Manager
Meryl Mason

Editorial Manager
Juliette Chambon

Editorial Assistants
Roxanne Rebours
Alexandre Hervé (intern)

Graphic design
Claire Luxey

Copyediting & proofreading
Myriam Birch

Colour separation
Litho Art New, Turin

Cover:
Songs of Home, 2021,
fabric, paper and acrylic on canvas,
96 × 120 in.

Crédits photographiques/Photographic credits
p. 17: © Photo courtesy of the Fowler Museum at UCLA
p. 21: © Frank Ugiomoh
p. 140: © Ayobami Ogungbe